THE CONQUEST

OF THE ILLINOIS

The Conquest

Of The Illinois

BY GEORGE ROGERS CLARK

EDITED BY

MILO MILTON QUAIFE

Editor of
The State Historical Society of wisconsin

KALPAZ

ISBN: 978-93-5128-966-1(PB)

First Published in 1920
Indian Reprint in 2017

Published by

Kalpaz Publications
C-30, Satyawati Nagar,
Delhi – 110052
E-mail: kalpaz@hotmail.com
Website: kalpazpublications.com
Ph.: +91-9212142040

Publishers' Preface

THE publishers of The Lakeside Classics have held themselves free to take any material that comes to hand, which promises to be interesting and worth while, regardless of its chronological relation to previous volumes, and this year they turn back from the early years of the Nineteenth Century to the stirring period of the Revolution.

Most of us think of the Revolution as being fought only in the Colonies stretched along the Atlantic Seaboard. Yet out in what is now Illinois and Indiana, a frontiersman by the name of George Rogers Clark carried on a campaign for American supremacy that for enterprise, daring and determination, is equal to any in our history. To his foresight and success is due the fact that the great country lying west of Pittsburgh, north of the Ohio and stretching to the Mississippi, was saved for the Colonies, and did not fall to the lot of Canada under the Treaty of Paris.

Clark's Memoir was written in illiterate style and with the spelling and punctuation of the frontiersman, and, in its original form, makes difficult reading for any but the historical scholar. We are, therefore, indebted to Mr.

Publishers' Preface

Milo M. Quaife not only for his continuing to act as editor, but also for his appreciation of the necessity of transcribing the Memoir and for accomplishing it so successfully.

The publishers feel that they are especially fortunate in being able to put this heroic, in readable form, into the hands of their friends and patrons, and do so with their annual message of Christmas Good-Will.

THE PUBLISHERS.

CHRISTMAS 1920.

Historical Introduction

Historical Introduction

By far the most brilliant figure in the Revolution in the West was George Rogers Clark, whose conquest of the Illinois country was the factor chiefly responsible for giving the Old Northwest to the new-born American nation in the treaty of 1783. To orient Clark's conquest in its historical setting, and to give some account of his narrative of it, which forms the subject-matter of the present volume, is the purpose of this introduction.

The region between the Ohio River and the Great Lakes, the Alleghenies and the Mississippi, which later became known as the Old Northwest, is the territory involved in our story. The beginning of the Revolution found the British, of course, in possession of all of it. The vantage points from which they directed its affairs were, in general, the old French posts, now occupied for the most part by British garrisons. Among these may be named Detroit, Mackinac, Vincennes, Kaskaskia, and Cahokia. By far the most important center of British influence in the Northwest was Detroit, the headquarters of the posts and the key to the control of the fur trade and the Indian tribes of this region. Here was a French and mixed-blood settlement numbering upwards of 2000 souls and mustering over 300 men capable of bearing arms. The fort was defended by a palisade of pickets and contained at the beginning of 1776 a garrison of 120 men. To complete the tale of Detroit's military resources, there floated in the river opposite the fort a tiny navy manned by some thirty "seamen and servants."

Detroit aside, the only other considerable centers of white population in the Northwest were Ouiatanon and Vincennes on the Wabash and the strip of settlements stretched along the east bank of the Mississippi from the mouth of the Missouri to the mouth of the Ohio, on what later came to be known as the "American Bottom." Ouiatanon had, at the outbreak of the Revolution, about a dozen French families. Vincennes had a population of perhaps 500 souls. The Illinois settlements of the American Bottom in 1778 contained about 1000 whites and as many negroes and Indians. The chief town was Kaskaskia with 500 white inhabitants and about the same number of negroes. Next in importance was Cahokia with a white population of about three hundred. At Mackinac and Green Bay, possibly also at St. Joseph, Peoria, and Prairie du Chien, were settled a few French families. For the rest, the country which now teems with a population as enlightened and prosperous as any on the face of the earth was but a splendid wilderness.

Scarcely second to the whites in importance, at least from the military point of view, was the Indian population of this region. The several tribes could muster, according to the usual estimates, about 8000 warriors. These were the jury, so to speak, to which the contending white leaders made their appeals, and on whose active aid or passive sympathy they relied as the makeweight to turn the scale in their favor. Most numerous of the tribes was the Chippewa; but our present concern lies rather with certain of the smaller tribes. Around the south end of Lake Michigan, with their principal seat on the St. Joseph River, were the Potawatomi, numbering some 400 warriors. To the south and southeastward of this tribe, in modern Indiana and Ohio, were the Miami, Shawnee, and others, who were to continue the war in the West during long and bloody years after the withdrawal of Great Britain from the contest. At Milwaukee had congregated a nondescript band composed of the off-scourings of several tribes, who, to the scandal of the British officers, usually maintained friendly relations with the Americans. In Illinois and Wisconsin were the Sauk and Foxes, the Winnebago, and other tribes.

The advancing wave of English settlement pouring into the upper Ohio Valley had precipitated, two decades earlier, the French and Indian War. As yet this tidal wave of civilization had not crossed the Ohio, although it had spread out along its eastern valley as far south as Tennessee. The most important post along this extensive frontier was Fort Pitt at the forks of the Ohio. It was the center, therefore, from which radiated the American efforts to control the Northwestern tribes, just as at a later date, it afforded the principal gateway through which the tide of settlement poured into this region.

The Americans at first strove to secure the neutrality of the Indians in the impending conflict. But the red man could not stand idly by while a war was waging for the possession of his country, and the British more wisely directed their efforts to securing his active support. This policy was shortly copied by the Americans, and soon the perplexed natives were being plied with rival solicitations for alliance. The British urged them to assail the outlying settlements of the American frontier, counselling humanity to the vanquished but largely nullifying this counsel by offering rewards for all scalps brought in. Lieutenant-Governor Hamilton at Detroit was especially zealous in urging the Indians on to this work of devastation. The Americans offered rewards for prisoners, but none for scalps.

Two courses of action were open to the Americans in view of this situation. They might endeavor to punish the hostile Indians by launching retaliatory measures against them; or they might by capturing Detroit, from whence issued alike the supplies for the marauders and the zeal which instigated them to their bloody task, destroy the opposition at its fountain-head. The latter course was urged by Colonel Morgan, the Indian agent for the Middle Department and a man of much experience among the Indians of the Northwest. The reasons advanced by him in support of the policy he advocated were unheeded. Seeing this, and believing a general Indian war was about to be precipitated, he resigned his office. The control of the Western Department passed into less competent hands and the western frontier seemed about to be overrun by the British and Indians when a diversion of much importance occurred. The advent of George Rogers Clark in the Illinois country compelled the British at Detroit to turn their attention to the defense of the Northwest, and shortly of Detroit itself, against the bold invader.

Clark was a native of Virginia who, like Washington, fitted himself for a surveyor and began his active career in the upper Ohio country. In 1776 he had cast in his lot with the young settlements of Kentucky, and although not yet twenty-five years of age, in the crisis of their fortune he put himself forward as their leader. The Kentucky settlements were nominally a part of Virginia but in fact they were too remote from the mother country to receive much protection from that source. It was congenial, too, to the spirit of the frontiersman to depend upon himself, and Clark, who had come to the conclusion that the only means of obtaining safety for Kentucky was to carry the war into the enemy's country, was one of those who favored action independently of authorization from Virginia.

Other counsels prevailed, however. The protection of the parent colony was sought and as a result the Virginia Assembly declared the extension of its authority over the region and in December, 1776, created the county of Kentucky. The next summer Clark learned from spies whom he had sent into the Illinois country that the French settlers were lukewarm in their allegiance to Great Britain and that only a few of them were participating in the raids against the Americans, which, fomented from Detroit, made these settlements their starting-point and base of operations. Fired by these reports with the purpose to conquer the Illinois settlements, he proceeded the same summer to Virginia. There he laid his project before Governor Henry and received that official's authorization to raise and equip a force of troops for the work. Armed with this and a scanty supply of money and ammunition he returned to Kentucky and launched the enterprise.

There is no need here to tell the story of Clark's invasion of the Illinois in the months of 1778 and 1779, for Clark's own narrative of his momentous campaign is spread before the reader in the pages that follow. Suffice it to say, therefore, that the morning of February

25, 1779, witnessed the climax of the campaign in the surrender to Clark at Vincennes of Lieutenant-Governor Hamilton and his entire garrison. Therewith the American hold on the Illinois country was assured, for the time being at least. Permanent control of the Northwest, and peace for the troubled frontier, could be won only by the capture of Detroit, and this was at all times the ultimate goal of Clark's endeavors. But he was too weak to move upon Detroit at once after the capture of Vincennes; while waiting for reinforcements he applied himself vigorously to the work of governing the newly-won territory, establishing satisfactory relations with the Indians and preparing the way for the greater exploit which he was destined never to perform. Obstacle after obstacle arose to postpone or prevent the fulfillment of his design. The British again resumed the offensive and the season of 1780 witnessed a comprehensive attack upon the American and Spanish positions in the West. A large force of traders and Indians which descended the Mississippi and fell upon St. Louis was repulsed and forced to beat a hasty retreat. Another British-Indian army under Captain Bird made a descent upon the Kentucky settlements, destroying Ruddle's and Martin's stations and carrying off to Detroit upwards of one hundred captives. The magic of Clark's name seems to have been a potent influence in causing the withdrawal from St.

Louis. He retaliated upon the invaders with vigor, sending a force of 350 men under Colonel Montgomery to ravage the villages of the Sauk and Foxes on Rock River, who had been active allies of the British. Himself hastening back to Kentucky upon the news of the British attack in that quarter, Clark organized a force of 1000 men for the punishment of the Shawnee, who had participated in the recent invasion of Kentucky. From the mouth of Licking River, opposite the present city of Cincinnati, the army proceeded to the Indian towns of Old Chillicothe and Piqua and burned the one, which had been abandoned, and stormed and burned the other. Although the issue of the campaign was not decisive, the punishment accorded the Indians sufficed to free the Kentucky settlements from further molestation by them for the remainder of the year 1780.

For the year 1781 plans were conceived on a large scale by Clark, Governor Jefferson of Virginia, and General Washington for the reduction of Detroit, but the settlers of western Pennsylvania and Virginia largely refused to respond to the call for troops; discord developed, too, between Clark and Colonel Brodhead, the American commander at Pittsburgh, and the settlers of Kentucky were either unequal or unwilling to undertake the task to which Clark eagerly invited them. So the matter dragged on and the Revolution finally came to its close with the British still in control at Detroit, whence they still continued to exert an effective control over most of the tribes of the Northwest. Not until a dozen years more of bloodshed along the Ohio frontier, concluding with the most serious Indian war in which the American nation has ever engaged, was the grip of Great Britain relaxed, and peace restored to the long-troubled frontier. The army of Mad Anthony Wayne triumphantly concluded the contest for the control of the Northwest which Clark almost twenty years earlier had so brilliantly begun.

With this hasty résumé of the military situation in the West we may turn to a consideration of Clark's story of his invasion of the Illinois. In the autumn of 1779 Clark prepared, in the form of a letter to his friend, George Mason of Virginia, a somewhat lengthy sketch of his Illinois campaign. With the passage of years the whereabouts of this letter became lost to knowledge and when, in the summer of 1789, at the instance of James Madison, Clark was urged to write out the story of his western campaigns for the benefit of posterity, he sought in vain to find the document. Nevertheless in response to much urging Clark set about composing a new narrative of the period, the resultant product being the famous memoir reproduced in the following pages. The original document is a manuscript of 128 pages, at least 100 of which were written during the years 1789 and 1790. For half a century, beginning with Mann Butler's *History of Kentucky*, published in 1834, historians generally regarded and utilized the *Memoir* as a trustworthy narrative of events, while such novelists as Winston Churchill in *The Crossing* and Maurice Thompson in *Alice of Old Vincennes* drew heavily upon it for the substance of their volumes. Theodore Roosevelt, however, in his *Winning of the West* vigorously questioned the value hitherto accorded to Clark's narrative. He supposed it to have been written "thirty or forty years" after the events described, and "by an old man who had squandered his energies and sunk into deserved obscurity." On the painful period of Clark's later years, here alluded to, there is no present necessity for entering. It is sufficient for our present purpose to note that the strictures of Roosevelt induced Professor James, the scholarly editor of Clark's *Papers* in the *Illinois Historical Collections*, to undertake a careful examination of the entire subject. His study established the fact, already noted, that the *Memoir* was chiefly written in 1789 and 1790, when Clark was still in full possession of his mental and physical powers; and led to the conclusion that the *Memoir*, far from being "the reminiscences of an old man who strove for the dramatic in his presentation of facts," is to be regarded as a generally trustworthy and highly valuable historical narrative of the events with which it deals.

Historical Introduction

With our faith in the narrative thus reëstablished, it remains for those who have a fondness for our western history to enjoy it. Unfortunately, from the viewpoint of the average man, as contrasted with the professional scholar, Clark's mastery of the pen by no means equalled his facility in the use of the sword. His education, viewed in the light of present-day standards, was necessarily defective. Even the trained scholar at times finds his efforts to determine Clark's meaning baffled, and it is probably safe to say that, professional scholars aside, very few persons have ever had the interest or perserverance to read the *Memoir* through. For such a document to remain comparatively unknown to the great mass of people in whose behalf Clark labored, is a great pity. Accordingly the effort has been made to give it an increased measure of publicity by reprinting in *The Lakeside Classics*. This determined upon, it seemed clear that instead of reprinting the *Memoir* literally the editor should undertake to turn it into clear and grammatical English. Such a reprint will not interest the professional scholar, of course, but for him there is already ample accommodation in the *George Rogers Clark Papers* published by the Illinois Historical Society, and W. H. English's *Conquest of the Country Northwest of the River Ohio*. If the present rendering awakens in the constituency of *The Lakeside*

Classics a renewed appreciation of the toils by which our country was won, and therewith an increased sense of its value to us, the present possessors, the hopes alike of publisher and editor will have been realized.

MILO M. QUAIFE.

Madison, Wisconsin.

The Conquest *of* The Illinois

The Conquest of The Illinois

SIR:

IN fulfilling my engagement to you with respect to the war in Kentucky I must commence with the first settlement of that district, which had been but partially explored prior to the year 1773, when a considerable number of surveyors and private adventurers passed through it. The first settlement was that of Harrodsburg, undertaken by Colonel J. Harrod[1] in the spring of 1774. Before much progress had been made, however, the settlers

[1]James Harrod was a native and resident of Pennsylvania who in March, 1774, advertised that he would lead a party to take up lands in Kentucky, which he had visited the preceding year. About thirty men assembled at his call and this party he piloted down the Ohio to the mouth of the Kentucky and up that stream and the Licking to the site of Harrodsburg. The war between the American settlers commonly known as Lord Dunmore's War of 1774 was about to break out, and before launching it two hardy woodsmen, Daniel Boone and Michael Stoner, were sent out as runners to Kentucky to warn the surveyors and other white men in that region of the impending conflict. At their warning the infant settlement of Harrodsburg was abandoned, and the settlers returned to the older Holston settlement. The year following Harrod returned to Kentucky, re-established Harrodsburg, and made the place his home until his death in 1793.

were compelled to abandon the country on account of the war with the Shawnee. They marched through the wilderness and joined Colonel Lewis' army,[2] but at the close of the war they returned and resumed possession of their town in the spring of 1775. In the meanwhile Colonel Henderson[3] and company had purchased the Kentucky country from the Cherokee and made an establishment and opened a land office at Boonesborough, but with these circumstances you are well acquainted.

It was at this period that I first entertained the thought of concerning myself about the interest of this country. The proprietors at first took great pains to win the favor of the settlers, but too soon for their own self-interest they began to raise the prices on their lands, which gave rise to much complaint. A few gentlemen made some effort to persuade the people to pay no attention to them. I saw clearly that the proprietors were working their own ruin, that their greatest security lay in

[2] General Andrew Lewis, commander in the notable battle of Point Pleasant, where the Great Kanawha River empties into the Ohio, October 10, 1774. Lewis long played a prominent rôle on the Pennsylvania and Virginia frontiers. In 1775 his appointment was urged by Washington as commander-in-chief of the Continental army.

[3] Colonel Richard Henderson was a prominent citizen of North Carolina who, like Harrod, conceived a project of settlement in Kentucky. He organized the Transylvania Company, purchased a vast quantity

making it to the interest of the settlers to support their claim, and that their conduct would shortly exasperate the people and afford the opportunity to overthrow them.

I left the country in the fall of 1775 and returned the following spring. While in Virginia diverse opinions were held respecting Henderson's claim. Many thought it good, while others doubted whether Virginia could with propriety advance any pretensions to the country. This was what I wanted to know. I immediately formed the plan of assembling the settlers and persuading them to elect delegates to proceed to Virginia and treat with that state concerning the Kentucky country; if suitable conditions were secured we would declare ourselves citizens of that state; if not, we would establish an independent government and by giving away a large part of the lands, and making other disposition of the remainder,

of goods, and invited the Cherokee, who claimed the tract which Henderson proposed to settle, to hold a treaty with him on the Watauga River in March, 1775. Some twelve hundred natives assembled, and on March 17 the treaty was consummated. The Transylvania Company thereupon settled Boonesborough, opened a land office, and held one legislative session in Kentucky. Their claim was disputed, however, and in 1778 the Virginia legislature granted the company 200,000 acres of land on Green River by way of payment for the expense incurred in settling Kentucky. Henderson went out with the first group of settlers, and his journal is now preserved in the Draper collection at Madison, Wisconsin.

we could not only gain a large number of inhabitants but in large measure protect them.

To carry this project into effect I appointed a general meeting of the settlers at Harrodsburg June 6, 1776, giving out that something would be proposed to them which much concerned their interest. My reason for withholding information as to what I wished to be done was in part to prevent the settlers from dividing into parties on the subject, in part to insure a more general attendance, as every one would wish to know what was to be done. Unfortunately, it was late in the evening of the day appointed before I could get to the place. The people had been in some confusion, but had at length concluded that the design was simply to send delegates to Virginia with a petition praying the Assembly to accept them as such and to establish a county government, etc. The polls were opened before my arrival, and the settlers had entered into the election with such spirit and carried matters so far that I could not get them to alter the plan of delegates with petitions to that of deputies under the authority of the people. In short, I did not make much effort to bring this about. John Gabriel Jones and myself were elected as delegates, the papers were prepared, and in a few days we set out for Williamsburg. We hoped to arrive before the Assembly should adjourn, for there was great apprehension that the Indians, stirred up by the British, would shortly make an attack upon Kentucky, and no time ought to be lost in putting it in a state of defence.

Apprehending no immediate danger on the Wilderness Road,[4] Mr. Jones and I set out without waiting for other company. We soon had cause to repent our rashness, however, for on the second day we discovered alarming signs of Indians. On the third day Mr. Jones' horse gave out. With our few belongings on my horse, and in so hilly a country, it was impossible for two to ride at a time. The weather was very rainy. Our feet were wet continuously for three or four days and nights, and, not daring to make a fire to dry them, we both got what the hunters call "scald feet," a most shocking complaint. In this situation we traveled on, in greater torment than I have ever before or since experienced, hoping to get relief at the station in Powell's Valley, ten or twelve miles from Cumberland Gap.

Greatly to our disappointment, we found the place totally abandoned and partly burned down. My companion, being but little used to such

[4] Before the conclusion of his treaty with the Cherokee at Watauga in the spring of 1775, Henderson sent Daniel Boone with a company of woodsmen to open a road to the Kentucky River, a distance of some two hundred miles. This was the origin of the famous Wilderness Road, over which thousands of emigrants later poured into the West. Its interesting history is told by Archer B. Hulbert in *Boone's Wilderness Road* (Cleveland, 1903).

hardship, became greatly discouraged at this blow to our hopes. I encouraged him by representing the certainty of the settlers being at Martin's fort, about eight miles ahead, as I supposed the whole had embodied there. Although the danger was much greater than we had apprehended, we were now fully apprised of it, and if we could make out to walk through the woods, both of us riding where there was level ground, we could reach the place without any great risk. This we attempted, but in vain; we were obliged to keep to the road, for the one on foot could not endure the torture of walking through the thick woods. Hearing Indian guns frequently, we had hopes they were hunters from the station to which we were bound, but to our surprise we found on arrival that the fort had been abandoned for some time. There were a few human tracks which we knew to be Indian, as also the guns we had heard.

Our situation now appeared deplorable. The nearest inhabitants we knew were sixty miles away, we were unable to travel, and the Indians appeared to be in full possession of the surrounding country. We sat still for a few moments looking at each other, and I found myself reduced to a state of perfect despair. Mr. Jones asked me what we should do. I told him it was impossible to make the settlement in our present condition, while if we hid in the mountains and the weather continued wet our situation would become worse rather than better and we would perhaps perish; that we knew a party was to follow us from Kentucky in eight or ten days; that oil and ouse made of oak bark would cure our feet in a few days, and I thought our only possible plan was to take possession of the best cabin in the place, fortify ourselves in it, and burn down the rest of the fort; that there were plenty of hogs around the corn cribs, and with a few of them and a barrel of water and some corn we probably could stand a siege until relieved by the party we expected to follow us from Kentucky; that ten or twelve Indians could not drive us from the place, as I was well acquainted with them and knew they would not storm us at great disadvantage to themselves; that we were well armed, having a rifle, two case of good pistols, and a hangar; and that I was confident we could defend ourselves against a larger number of Indians than he had any idea of.

He was overjoyed at the proposition and we fell to work. I sent him to kill a hog which was eating corn, by running a sword through it to prevent noise. I selected a small strong cabin of Captain Martin's which stood a little detached from the rest. The door being locked with some tables and chairs inside, I climbed to the top of the chimney and flung it down until it was so low that I could drop into the house without hurting myself (not being able to support myself with my feet against the logs) and cut off the lock of the door. By this time my friend had got his hog. Being better able to walk, he filled a keg with water, and we collected some wood and brought in some corn. We then barred the door, knocked out some portholes, set the table in the middle of the floor and spread our arms and ammunition in order upon it, and waited impatiently for the wind to shift so that we might set fire to the fort without burning our own castle. Our agreement was that in case of an attack Mr. Jones should continue to load the pieces as I discharged them, without paying any attention to the enemy unless they stormed the house. We cooked some provisions, dressed our feet with oil, and continued diligently preparing for defense until late in the evening. Then, the wind having died away, we proposed to set fire to the houses as we had planned. We had no sooner unbarred the door, however, than we heard a horse bell open on the road and in a few minutes stop again. We were fully convinced that the enemy was at hand, and immediately secured ourselves as well as possible, determined to execute our first plan, and if they should attempt to burn us out to knock off the roof of the cabin. We waited in suspense for some time, but at last to our great joy we found they were white men who had come from the settlement on Clinch River to collect some things they had hid at the time they had left this place. When they came in sight of the fort the bell on one of their horses became untied. When they discovered the smoke of our fire, supposing us to be Indians, they approached under cover in order to discover the full situation and gain an advantage over us. While they were thus engaged we had a full view of them, and accordingly we disclosed ourselves to them. They appeared to be happy over having it in their power to relieve us, and we crossed the mountains with them to the settlements.

Having recruited our strength, we resumed our journey as far as Boutetourt County, and there learned we were too late for the Assembly, which had already adjourned. For some time we were at a loss to determine what our future course should be. We finally concluded to remain in Virginia until the fall session, and that in the meantime I should go to Williamsburg and endeavor to procure some, powder for the settlers in Kentucky, and in general look after their interests.

We parted. Mr. Jones returned to Holston, there to join the force that was being raised to repel the Cherokee, who had recently commenced hostilities, while I proceeded on my way. Governor Henry of Virginia lay sick at his home in Hanover, where I waited on him and presented my credentials. He appeared much disposed to favor the Kentuckians and gave me a letter to the Council on the subject. I waited upon that body. My application was for 500 pounds of powder to be conveyed to Kentucky for immediate use. After various questions had been asked, and consultations held, the Councillors agreed to furnish the powder; but as we were a detached people not yet united to the state of Virginia, and until the session of the Assembly it was uncertain whether we would become united, they could only lend us the ammunition as to friends in distress, and I must become responsible in case the Assembly should not receive us as citizens of the state. I informed them it was beyond my power to pay the expense of transporting and guarding these supplies. The British officers on our frontier were employing every energy to engage the Indians in the war. The settlers might be destroyed for want of this small supply, and I hoped they would reconsider the matter and do us the favor of sending us the ammunition at public expense. They replied that they were disposed to do for us everything in their power, consistent with their official duty, and this I believed to be true.

After advancing many arguments to convince me that even what they had proposed was a stretch of power, they informed me they could venture no further, and an order was issued to the keeper of the magazine to deliver the ammunition to me. For twelve months past I had reflected so much upon the several continental factors which affected us that my resolution was formed before I left the council chamber. I resolved to return the order I had received and repair immediately to Kentucky, knowing the settlers would readily adopt my first plan, as what had occurred had rendered its success practically certain. I wrote to the Council and enclosed the order for the powder. I told them I had weighed the matter and found it was out of my power to convey those stores at my own expense such a distance through a hostile country; that I was sorry to find that we would have to seek protection elsewhere, which I did not doubt of getting; and that if a country was not worth protecting it was not worth claiming. What transpired on the reception of this letter I do not know. I was now sent for by a set of gentlemen who were zealous in the welfare of their country, and I fully apprised them of the probable course of events in Kentucky. Being somewhat prejudiced in favor of my mother country, I was willing to meet them half way. Orders were immediately issued, dated August 23, 1776, for conveying the ammunition to Pittsburgh, there to await further orders from me.

Matters being thus amicably arranged, I wrote a letter informing the Kentuckians what had been done and recommending that they send to Pittsburgh for the powder and convey it by water to Kentucky, but they never received the letter. I myself remained in Virginia until the fall session, when I was joined by my colleague, Mr. Jones, and we laid our papers before the Assembly. That body decided that we could not take our seats as members, but that our business should be attended to. Colonel Henderson, one of the purchasers from the Cherokees, was present and greatly retarded our business. Colonel Arthur Campbell,[5] a member of the Assembly, also strongly opposed the project for a new county, wishing us to remain annexed to the county on whose frontier we lay and which he himself represented. This caused it to be late in the session before we secured the establishment of a new county by the name of Kentucky.

Mr. Jones and I parted at Williamsburg, but learning there that the ammunition was still at Pittsburgh, we resolved to return that way and take it down the river. We agreed to meet there, but the weather proving severe it was late in the fall before we could set out. However trifling a small quantity of ammunition

[5] Colonel Arthur Campbell was one of the prominent men of the Virginia border. At the age of fifteen he was captured by a band of Northwestern Indians and spent three years as a captive in the vicinity of Lake Erie. In 1765 his father settled on the Middle Fork of Holston in modern Smyth County. Here young Campbell built the first mill in 1770, served as justice of the peace, and took part in all the stirring events of the Virginia border in the following years. In 1780 he conducted a brilliant campaign against the Cherokee. The leadership at the famous battle of King's Mountain the following year he resigned to his cousin, William Campbell. He died near Middlesborough, Kentucky, in 1811.

or the loss or acquisition of a few men may appear to the country as a whole, I knew that by the Kentuckians the loss of either would be severely felt, and accordingly I exercised all possible care. I found the Indians to be fully prepared for war in the spring, and those who came in to Fort Pitt under color of friendship were in fact acting as spies: also that they suspected our intention of going down the river and would attempt to intercept us.

Realizing that our safety depended solely upon expedition, without waiting to recruit our party we set out with but seven hands in a small vessel, and by the most indefatigable labor accomplished our journey. We passed the Indians in the night, or by some other means got ahead of them, for the day before we landed at Limestone[6] we plainly discovered they were pursuing us. We hid our stores in four or five places, scattered at considerable distances, and, running a few miles farther down the river, turned our vessel adrift and set out by land for Harrodsburg to get an adequate force of men to return for the ammunition. We passed the Blue Licks[7] and on the third day

[6] Modern Maysville, long the chief river post for Kentucky.

[7] On Licking River. Here were noted salt deposits. While making salt here in 1778 Daniel Boone was captured by the Indians. In August, 1782, occurred here the disastrous battle of Blue Licks, wherein a large number of Kentucky frontiersmen were slain.

after leaving the river arrived at Hinkston's cabin[8] on the west fork of Licking Creek. While we were resting here four men who had been out looking up land in that section came up and informed us concerning the situation of affairs in Kentucky. They told us the late Colonel John Todd[9] was out with a party somewhere in the vicinity, and if we could find him we would be strong enough to return to the river. But whether we could find him was uncertain.

As several of our party were much fatigued, we agreed that I and two others should proceed to Harrodsburg for the proposed party, while Mr. Jones and the others should remain in that

[8] Major John Hinkston, a native of Pennsylvania, was a noted scout and woodsman who in 1775 led a company of settlers into Kentucky and erected a station near modern Paris. This was abandoned in July, 1776, through fear of Indian ravages. Four years later, Hinkston brought his family to Kentucky, but had just arrived at his old station when he was captured by a British-Indian force under Col. Henry Bird.

[9] John Todd was a native of Pennsylvania who was educated in Virginia. He practiced law for a time and in 1774 took part in the campaign against the Shawnee which ended in the battle of Point Pleasant. In 1775 he removed to Kentucky, served in the Transylvania legislature, and was one of the first delegates from Kentucky County to the Virginia legislature. After Clark's conquest of the Illinois country Todd was sent out to serve as county-lieutenant of the newly-organized county of Illinois. He held this office one year, when he returned to Kentucky. He was killed in the battle of the Blue Licks in 1782.

neighborhood until our return. Shortly after I had set out, however, Colonel Todd arrived at the place, and after some consultation concluded they were strong enough to go to the river and bring in the ammunition and other stores. Accordingly he set out with ten men, but on December 25, between the Licking and the Ohio, he met the Indians who were following our trail, and was totally routed. Mr. Jones was killed and three others were either killed or taken prisoners.[10] Fortunately for us, the prisoners did not reveal to the Indians our hidden stores.

On December 29th a large party of Indians attacked McClelland's Fort[11] on Elkhorn. They killed McClelland and White and wounded two others, after which the survivors moved to Harrodsburg. The inhabitants of Kentucky at this period consisted of about men in

[10] One of those thus captured was Joseph Rogers, a cousin of Clark. He was held in captivity several years. At length when Clark led his expedition against the Shawnee towns of Ohio in the summer of 1780, Rogers found his opportunity to escape. In the fighting which attended Clark's capture of Piqua, he ran towards the Americans, shouting to them not to shoot him for he was a white man. He fell mortally wounded, however, and expired a short time after Clark reached his side.

[11] McClelland's station had been established late in 1775 or early in 1776 near the site of modern Georgetown. The attack here noted was made by Captain Pluggy's band of Indians. Pluggy was himself slain in this attack.

the stations of Harrodsburg, Boonesborough. and Colonel Logan's (station),[12] which had been established about this time. The information I gave sufficiently alarmed them. The settlers had scarcely time enough to prepare themselves when a large body of Indians advanced, on March 7, 1777, (on the 5th the militia of the city had been embodied), to the attack on Harrodsburg. They fired on some boys in the evening five miles from town, killing one of them. The others made their escape and gave the alarm. A party from the fort advanced to the place, but fortunately, it being late in the evening, they did not fall in with the Indians, as in all probability our party would have been cut to pieces and of course the country lost. The loss of a single man at this time was sensibly felt, and general actions with the enemy must be avoided except when we had an evident superiority, as the enemy could easily retrieve their losses by recruits from numerous tribes, an advantage we could not expect to enjoy for some time.

On the following morning the Indians entered the upper part of the town (which had been evacuated the evening before), and a little

[12] Logan's station, about ten miles from Boonesborough, was established in 1775. Its founder, Benjamin Logan, was a native of Virginia who bore a prominent part in the development of Kentucky. He was a noted Indian fighter, and served in numerous campaigns of this period. He died in Shelby County in 1802.

after daylight set fire to one of the houses. A small party of men immediately went to see what was the cause of this and were fired upon by the Indians. However, they were covered by a party from the fort and made good their retreat. In this affair one man was killed on each side, and a few were wounded.

Being the superior officer, I had the country put into as good a state of defense as our situation would admit, determined if possible to stand our ground in hopes of relief, as the governor of Virginia had uniformly appeared to be our friend. From this period we may date the commencement of that bloody war in Kentucky which has continued with savage fury ever since. Upward of two thousand souls have perished on our side, in a moderate calculation, and the war has been severely felt by the most active Indian nations. It is impossible to enumerate all the little actions that took place. They were continual, and frequently severe when compared to our small forces. The forts were frequently attacked. Good policy would seem to have required that the whole force be embodied in one place, but our dependence upon hunting for the greatest portion of our provisions forbade this. No people could be in a more alarming position. Detached at least two hundred miles from the nearest settlement of the states, we were surrounded by numerous Indian nations, each one far superior to ourselves in numbers and spurred on by the British government to destroy us, as appeared from many instruments of writing left us on the breasts of persons killed by them.

I frequently feared the settlers would consider making peace with Detroit and suffer themselves and families to be carried off. Their distress may be easily conceived from our situation; yet they remained firm in the hope of relief, which they received by the arrival of a company of men under Colonel John Bowman[13] on the second of September. This reinforcement, though small, gave an appearance of new life to the situation. Encouraged by this and by the stand they had already made, every one seemed determined to exert himself in strengthening the country by encouraging as many of his friends to move out, and in the end this measure was successful. After the arrival of Colonel Bowman I left Kentucky, in October, 1777, and returned to Virginia with a party of young men who had been detained on the promise of being liberated upon his arrival. During the severe spring preceding,

[13] Colonel John Bowman, a native of Virginia, visited Kentucky in 1775. The following summer he was at Harrodsburg, where he served on the committee of safety. In the autumn of 1776 he was chosen colonel of Kentucky militia, and led thither a company for the defense of the settlers, arriving in August, 1777. In 1779 he led an expedition into the Miami country, but nothing decisive was accomplished. He died in Lincoln County, Kentucky, in 1784.

our conduct had been very uniform. The defense of our forts, the procuring of provisions, and when possible surprising the Indians (which was frequently done), burying the dead and dressing the wounded, seemed to comprise our entire business.

The whole of my time when not thus employed was devoted to reflecting upon things in general; particularly whether or no it accorded with the interest of the United States to support Kentucky. This led me to a long train of thinking, the result of which was to lay aside every private view and engage seriously in the war, having the interest and the welfare of the public my only concern until the fate of the continent should be known; divesting myself of prejudice and partiality in favor of any particular parts of the country, I determined to pursue what I considered to be the interest of the whole. This has influenced my conduct throughout the course of the war, and enabled me better to judge of the importance of Kentucky to the Union, situated as it was almost in the midst of the Indians, who had commonly engaged in the Kentucky war as an impediment in their way to the more interior frontiers. I saw that as soon as they should accomplish the destruction of Kentucky they would descend upon our frontiers; and instead of the states receiving supplies from thence, they would be obliged to keep large bodies of troops for their defense. It would be almost impossible to move an army at so great a distance to attack their towns, even if they could be found. By supporting Kentucky and encouraging its growth these obstacles would in great measure be removed; for should the British officers perceive their mistaken policy in carrying on the war against Kentucky by the Indians and, withdrawing from them, bend their whole force against the interior frontiers as a certain mode of distressing the states, we might, with a little assistance, march with ease at any time from this country to any part of their country we might choose. (This is the only circumstance that can excuse their conduct.)

These ideas caused me to view Kentucky in the most favorable point of view, as a place of the greatest consequence, which ought to meet with every encouragement, and to perceive that nothing I could engage in would be of more general utility than its defense. As I knew the commandant of the different towns of the Illinois country and the Wabash was busily engaged in exciting the Indians against us, their reduction became my first object. I sent two young hunters, S. Moore and B. Linn,[14] to those places as spies, with proper instructions

[14] These were Lieutenant Samuel Moore and Lieutenant Benjamin Linn. The latter was a younger brother of Colonel William Linn. He spent his early life in western Maryland, moving in 1769 to the Monongahela River. He went to Kentucky early in 1776 and the following spring was chosen a lieutenant of the Kentucky County militia. On the mission to

for their conduct. To prevent suspicion, neither they nor anyone in Kentucky knew anything of my design until it was ripe for execution. They returned to Harrodsburg with all the information I could reasonably have expected. I found by them that the Illinois people had but little expectation of a visit from us. Things were kept in good order, however, the militia trained, etc., that they might be prepared in case of a visit. I learned that the greatest pains were taken to inflame the minds of the French inhabitants against the Americans, notwithstanding which the spies had discovered traces of affection for us on the part of some of the inhabitants; and that the Indians from that region were generally engaged in the war upon us.

When I left Kentucky, October 1, 1777, I plainly saw that every eye was turned towards me as if expecting some stroke in their favor. Some of the settlers doubted my return, supposing I would join the army in Virginia: I left them with reluctance, promising (what I had predetermined) that I would certainly return to their assistance.

Kaskaskia, here noted, he narrowly escaped detection, and retired in haste at the suggestion of a friend to the Americans. He did not go on Clark's expedition against Kaskaskia, but in 1779 he joined him at Vincennes. He later became a somewhat noted Baptist preacher, and founded the second church of that denomination in Kentucky. He died at Huntsville, Alabama, in December, 1814.

On my arrival at Williamsburg I remained a considerable time settling the accounts of the Kentucky militia and taking note of everything I saw or heard that shed light on the disposition of those in power. Burgoyne's army having been captured and things seeming to wear a pleasing aspect, on December 10 I communicated my design to Governor Henry. At first he seemed to favor it, but to send a party off to so great a distance appeared daring and hazardous even though the service to be performed might be of great utility. To lay the matter before the Assembly, then in session, would be dangerous, as it would soon be known throughout the frontiers, and the first prisoner taken by the Indians would probably give the alarm, which would end in the certain destruction of the party. Governor Henry therefore held several private councils with select men. After making every inquiry into my proposed plans of operations (and particularly into that of a retreat in case of misfortune, in which event I intended to cross the Mississippi into Spanish territory) the expedition was resolved upon; and as an encouragement to those who would engage in it a document was drawn up whereby those gentlemen promised, in the event of success, to use their influence to procure from the Assembly 300 acres of land for each man.

The Governor and Council entered so warmly into the enterprise that I had very little trouble in getting matters adjusted, and on January 2, 1778, I received my instructions. I received also £1200 for the use of the expedition and an order on the authorities at Pittsburgh for boats, ammunition, etc. Finding from the Governor's conversation with me upon the subject that he did not wish an implicit attention to his instructions should prevent my doing anything that would manifestly tend to the public advantage, I set out on January 4, clothed with all the authority I could wish. I advanced £150 to Major William B. Smith[15] to recruit a force of men on Holston and meet me in Kentucky. Captain Leonard Helm[16] of Fauquier

[15] William Bailey Smith, a native of Virginia, who early migrated to North Carolina, where he associated with the Hendersons and other prominent men of the time. In 1775 he attended the treaty at Watauga whereby Henderson secured his Kentucky claim from the Cherokee, and he went out to Boonesborough that summer. In 1777 he went back to the settlements and brought out a force of men for the relief of Kentucky. He largely failed in his recruiting efforts for which Clark commissioned him. Of the one small company he eventually forwarded to Clark, a portion deserted on learning the destination of the expedition. Smith later returned to North Carolina where he was commissioned to extend the boundary line between modern Tennessee and Kentucky. For this service he received a tract on Green River, where he settled in 1794 and died in 1818.

[16] Leonard Helm had served with Clark in Lord Dunmore's War of 1774. He was one of Clark's captains in the Illinois expedition, and the commander relied more upon him, perhaps, than any other member of his force.

and Captain Bowman of Frederick were each to raise a company and arrive on February 1 at Redstone old fort.[17]

Being now in the country where all my arrangements were to be made, I appointed Captain William Harrod[18] and many other officers to the recruiting service and contracted for flour and other necessary stores. General Hand,[19] who

[17] This was at the mouth of Redstone Creek, where the Ohio Company had built a storehouse as early as 1752. In 1754 the English defenses here were burned by the French, but after the capture of Fort Duquesne by the English in 1758, an officer was sent to reëstablish a fort at this point. It was abandoned during Pontiac's War, but appears to have been garrisoned at the time of Lord Dunmore's War in 1774, and was now made the rendezvous for Clark's forces. In 1785 the town of Brownsville was incorporated here, and this remained for many years an important starting point for western emigration.

[18] This was the elder brother of James Harrod, the founder of Harrodsburg. William was with his brother at this place in 1775, but western Pennsylvania continued to be his permanent home. He raised a company under the appointment from Clark here noted and, joining his commander at the Falls of Ohio, served efficiently throughout the Illinois campaign. The next year he brought a company from the Falls of Ohio to take part in Colonel Bowman's campaign into the Miami country in 1779. He died in 1801.

[19] Edward Hand was born in Ireland on the last day of the year 1744. He studied medicine and in 1767 became surgeon's mate in the British army, his regiment being sent to America that same summer. It was at once ordered to Fort Pitt, where Hand served until 1774; then, the regiment being ordered east, he

then commanded at Pittsburgh, promised a supply of the articles for which I had orders. I received word from Captain Helm that several gentlemen in his section were endeavoring to counteract his efforts at recruiting, saying no such service was known to the Assembly. In consequence he had to send to the Governor to have his conduct ratified. I also encountered opposition to our enterprise in the country around Pittsburgh, where the people were violently divided into parties over the territorial claims of Virginia and Pennsylvania. As my real instructions were kept secret and only an instrument prepared by the Governor designedly for deception and directing me to raise men for the defense of Kentucky was made public, many men of both parties considered it injurious to the public interest to draw off men at so critical a moment for the defense of a few detached inhabitants that had better be removed.

These circumstances caused some confusion in the business of recruiting. On March 29 I

resigned and settled at Lancaster, Pennsylvania. At the outbreak of the Revolution he enlisted in the colonial army and soon joined Washington before Boston, serving later in the Long Island and New Jersey campaigns. In the spring of 1777 he was made brigadier-general and sent to the West as commander-in-chief. Hampered here in his work, he asked to be recalled early the following year, and served in the East until the close of the war. He then retired to his home near Lancaster and resumed the practice of medicine. He died September 3, 1802.

received a letter from Major Smith by express informing me that he had raised four companies on Holston ready to march immediately to Kentucky in accordance with his orders; while an express from Kentucky brought information that they had been much strengthened since I left there. This information concerning Smith's four companies, besides those of Bowman and Helm which I knew were on their way to join me at Redstone, made me feel easier on the subject of recruits than I otherwise would have been. The recruiting officers secured only such men as had friends in Kentucky or were induced by a desire to see the country.

Meeting with several disappointments, it was late in May before I could leave Redstone with three companies of men and a considerable number of families and private adventurers. Taking in my stores at Pittsburgh and Wheeling, I proceeded cautiously down the Ohio. At the mouth of the Great Kanawha Captain Arbuckle,[20] the commandant, informed us that 250 Indians had warmly attacked his post the day before and wounded a few of his men. The Indians had then directed their course to the

[20] Captain Matthew Arbuckle was one of the best known woodsmen and Indian fighters of this period. In 1765 he had explored the Kanawha Valley to the Ohio, the first white man to pass this way except as a captive in the hands of the Indians. In 1776 he was sent to command Fort Randolph at the mouth of the Kanawha, where he remained for the three ensuing years. He was killed in 1781 by a falling tree.

settlements of Greenbrier and Captain Arbuckle had sent off an express to warn the settlers. He thought the forces I had, with the addition of a part of a garrison, could in all probability overtake the Indians and inflict a total rout upon them. The prospect was a flattering one; but the uncertainty of obtaining the advantage over the enemy, the loss of time and perhaps a number of the men, which would cause the destruction of the enterprise upon which I had embarked — these considerations, together with the practical certainty that the settlers would receive the alarm in time and might repel the invaders (which they in fact did), induced me to decline it.

I proceeded on my way, therefore, being joined by Captain James O'Hara,[21] who was on his way to the Arkansas on public business. I landed at the mouth of the Kentucky River.

[21]James O'Hara entered the Indian trade at Pittsburgh prior to 1773. He enlisted in the Ninth Virginia Regiment during the Revolution, being employed as quartermaster. In the Whiskey Rebellion of Washington's administration he served as quartermaster-general of the army, and in a similar capacity under General Wayne in 1794. In 1797 he established at Pittsburgh the first glass manufactory west of the Alleghanies, and by his business ability did much to develop the town. He died in 1819 leaving a large estate. At the time of Clark's journey O'Hara had been sent by General Hand to succor Captain Willing, who had gone to the lower Mississippi country to secure the neutrality of the inhabitants there and bring back provisions to the states. Willing, although

Here I had intended to erect a fort, since the growth of Kentucky largely depended upon the establishment of a post on the Ohio River as a place of security for emigrants who wished to descend the river; but having in view my designs to the westward I perceived the mouth of the Kentucky was not a proper place to fortify unless we could afford to maintain two posts. In case of success attending my enterprise it would be absolutely necessary to have a post of communication on the river between the Illinois country and Kentucky; and of course the Falls of Ohio[22] was the more eligible spot as it would answer all these desirable purposes and would also protect in great measure the navigation of the river, since as every vessel would be obliged to stop some time at this place they would always be exposed to the Indians.

not mentioned by Clark, is of interest to our story in at least two respects. After a long and stormy career in the far Southwest, he sent his troops up the Mississippi, under charge of Lieutenant Robert George, who, arriving in the Illinois country, placed them subject to the orders of Clark. Willing himself went to Mobile where he was captured by the British and narrowly escaped being hung. After a long imprisonment, at one time being loaded with irons in New York City for three months, Willing was released on parole and finally exchanged for Governor Henry Hamilton, who since his capture by the Americans had undergone ill treatment at their hands fairly comparable to that which the British meted out to Willing.

[22] At the site of modern Louisville.

I had learned that but one company of Major Smith's troops, that of Captain Dillard, had as yet arrived in Kentucky. This alarmed me, as I feared the disappointment would prove fatal to our enterprise. I wrote a letter to Colonel Bowman telling him of my intention to place a garrison at the Falls, and that I had an object in view of greatest importance to the country. I urged him to meet me there with the available troops recruited by Major Smith and what militia could safely be spared from the different posts.

I moved on the Falls and inspected the several sites available for fortifying; but reflecting that my secret instructions were as yet unknown even to my own party, and not knowing what would be the consequence when they should be divulged, I wished to have everything as secure as possible when we should be joined by the entire force. I observed that the little island of about seven acres opposite the present site of Louisville was seldom or never entirely covered by water. I resolved to take possession and fortify it which I did on the of June, dividing the island among the families that had followed me, for gardens. These families I now found to be a real asset, as they occasioned but little expense and with the invalids would hold this little post until we should be able to occupy the mainland. This last occurred in the fall agreeably to instructions I sent from the Illinois. The people on the

Monongahela, learning of this post by messengers I sent to them, moved down the river in great numbers. This was one of the chief causes of the rapid settlement of Kentucky.

Upon the arrival of Colonel Bowman with part of the militia and several gentlemen of this section of country we found on examination that we were much weaker than I had expected to be; meanwhile the Indians continued their warfare without intermission and their numbers increased the longer they continued, as the British steadily added to their strength by stirring up others to join them. Under these circumstances we could not think of leaving the posts of Kentucky defenseless. We perceived that it was better to run a great risk with one party than to divide our forces in such a manner as to hazard the loss of both. We therefore agreed to take but one complete company and part of another from Kentucky, supposing that these would be replaced by troops we yet expected from Major Smith.

Such were our deliberations after I had made known my instructions. Almost every gentleman present warmly espoused the enterprise and plainly saw the utility of it, and supposed they saw the salvation of Kentucky almost within their reach, but they sorely repined that we were not strong enough to put it beyond all doubt. The soldiery in general debated on the subject but determined to follow their officers. Some were alarmed at the thought of being taken so great a distance into the enemy's country, fearing that even though they should be successful in the first instance they might be attacked in their posts without the possibility of obtaining succor or of making their retreat. I had spies continually among them, and some dissatisfaction was discovered in Captain Dillard's company. The boats were well secured, therefore, and sentinels were placed where it was thought there was a possibility of the men wading from the island. My design was to take those who would not attempt to desert down the river on our way,[23] but I was outgeneraled by Lieutenant , of whom I had previously conceived a very tolerable opinion. While swimming during the day, they discovered that the channel opposite their camp might be waded, and a little before daybreak he and the greater part of the company slipped down the bank and reached the opposite shore before they were discovered by the sentinels.

Vexed at the idea of their escape in this manner, since one of my principal motives for taking my station on the island was to prevent desertion, and intending to set out the next day, I was undetermined for a few moments what to do. It might require several days for a party to overtake the deserters and having no distrust of those that remained the example was not immediately dangerous.

[23] The precise meaning which Clark intended to convey by this statement is not clear.

However it might prove so hereafter, and recalling that we had with us a number of horses belonging to the gentlemen from Harrodsburg, I ordered a strong party to pursue them; the foot and horse were to relieve each other regularly, and they were to put to death every man they could who would not surrender. They overhauled the deserters in about twenty miles. The latter, discovering their pursuers at a distance, scattered in the woods and only seven or eight were taken. The remainder made their way to different posts; many who were not woodsmen almost perished. The poor lieutenant and the few that remained with him, after suffering almost all that could be felt from hunger and fatigue, arrived at Harrodsburg, where the settlers, having heard of his conduct, would not for some time suffer him to come into their houses nor give him anything to eat. On the return of the party the soldiery hung and burned his effigy.

Every preparation was now made for our departure. After spending a day of amusement we parted with our friends from Kentucky, they to return to the defense of their country and we in search of new adventures. On the twenty-fourth of June, 1778, we left our little island and running about a mile up the river in order to gain the main channel, we shot the Falls at the very moment the sun was under a great eclipse, which caused various conjectures on the part of the superstitious among us.

Knowing that spies were watching the river below the Illinois towns, I had planned to march part of the way by land. I therefore left behind all of our baggage except enough to equip the men after the Indian fashion. Our entire force, after leaving behind those who were judged unequal to the expected fatigues of the march, consisted of but four companies, under Captains Montgomery, Bowman, Helm, and Harrod. My force being so much smaller than I had expected, I found it necessary to alter my plan of operations. As Vincennes was a town of considerable strength, having four hundred militia, besides which there was an Indian town adjoining and large numbers of Indians always in the neighborhood, and since it was more important than any other from the viewpoint of Indian affairs, I had thought of attacking it first; but I now found myself too weak to undertake this, and accordingly resolved to begin operations against the Illinois towns. Although they had more inhabitants than Vincennes they were scattered in different villages. There was less danger of our being immediately overpowered by the Indians; in case of necessity, too, we could probably make good our retreat to the Spanish side of the river, while if we were successful here the way might be paved for us to take possession of Vincennes.

I was well aware of the fact that the French inhabitants of these western settlements had great influence over the Indians, by whom they were more beloved than were any other Europeans. I knew also that their commercial intercourse extended throughout the entire western and northwestern country, while the governing interest on the Great Lakes was chiefly in the hands of the English, who were not popular with the natives. These reflections, along with others of similar import, determined me to strengthen myself, if possible, by adopting such a course of conduct as would tend to attach the whole French and Indian population to our interest, and give us influence beyond the limits of the country which constituted the objective of our campaign. Such were the principles which guided my further conduct; fortunately I received at this time a letter from Colonel Campbell[24] at Pittsburgh informing me of the contents of the treaty between France and America.

[24] Colonel John Campbell was a native of Ireland who early came to America and entered upon the Indian trade. In 1764 he laid out a town on the site of modern Pittsburgh, and ten years later purchased a large tract of land at the Falls of Ohio. He acted as commissary at Fort Pitt during the early years of the Revolution. In the summer of 1779 he was captured at the defeat of Colonel Rogers' party on the Ohio a short distance above Cincinnati. Campbell was carried to Quebec and there held prisoner until almost the close of the Revolution. In 1784 he located in the vicinity of Louisville. He served in the Virginia legislature from Kentucky, in the Kentucky constitutional convention of 1792, and in 1798 was speaker of the state senate. He died in 1799.

Intending to leave the Ohio at Fort Massac,[25] three leagues below the mouth of the Tennessee, I landed on Barataria, a small island in the mouth of that river, to make preparations for our march. A few hours after our arrival here, one John Duff, coming down the river with a party of hunters, was brought to by our boats. They were originally from the states, and they expressed pleasure in the adventure, their surprise having been owing to lack of knowledge who we were. They had recently been at Kaskaskia and were able to give us all the information we desired. They told us that Governor Abbott[26] had recently left Vincennes to go to Detroit on business of importance.

[25] Fort Massac was a French post erected in 1757 on the north side of the Ohio, eight miles below Paducah, Kentucky. When the French surrendered Illinois to the British the latter neglected to fortify this point, and so Clark was enabled to make it his point of entry into Illinois. In 1794 General Wayne established a fort on the site of the old French post, and the new Fort Massac continued for many years a post of the regular army in the Northwest.

[26] Edward Abbott was a British artillery officer who came into the Northwest about the close of the French regimé in this region. In the spring of 1777 he was sent to Vincennes, being the first and only British governor there. He built Fort Sackville, which Clark captured from Hamilton in the winter of 1779. As here noted, Abbott was withdrawn from Vincennes in February, 1778. In July of this year he was sent to the West Indies, and therewith ceased to figure in the history of the Northwest.

Mr. Rochblave[27] was commanding at Kaskaskia. The militia were in good order, spies were watching the Mississippi, and all hunters were instructed to keep close watch for the rebels. The fort was kept as orderly as an asylum, but our informants thought this watchfulness was due more to a fondness for parade than to any expectation of a visit from us. Should they receive timely notice of our approach, the hunters thought, they would give us a warm reception, since they had been taught to entertain horrible ideas of the barbarity of the rebels, especially so of the Virginians. If, however, we could surprise the place, they had no doubt of our ability to master it at pleasure.

These men asked to be permitted to join our expedition, and offered to assist the guides in conducting our party across the country. This offer was accepted by me and they proved a

[27] Philippe Francois Rastel, sieur de Rochblave, was a native of France who served for a time in the army. Coming to New France about the year 1750, he entered the colonial army and was employed about Fort Duquesne and in the Illinois country. At the close of the French and Indian War he located at Kaskaskia and here married in 1763. Later he crossed the Mississippi into Spanish territory and was at Ste. Genevieve, Missouri, for a time. In 1776, when the last British officer withdrew from Kaskaskia, Rochblave was left in command, but with no garrison or other support. Clark sent him a prisoner to Virginia. Here he evaded his parole and made his way to the British army in New York. He died in Lower Canada in 1802.

valuable acquisition, all the more so in view of the fact that I had had no intelligence concerning the French posts since that gained from the spies I had sent a year before. No part of the information I received pleased me more than that concerning the inhabitants believing us to be more savage than their neighbors, the Indians. I resolved to make capital of this should I be fortunate enough to gain control over them, since I considered that the greater the shock I could give them in the beginning the more appreciative would they be later of my lenity, and the more valuable as friends. This I conceived to accord with human nature as I had observed it in many instances.

All things being ready, we descended the river to a little gut a short distance above Fort Massac, where we concealed our boats and began our march in a northwesterly direction. Nothing worthy of remark occurred in this portion of our route. The weather was favorable, although in some places both water and game were scarce, which entailed some suffering both from thirst and hunger. On the third day John Saunders, our principal guide, appeared to be confused, and barring some other explanation of his conduct, we perceived that he was totally lost. I asked him a number of questions and was at a loss to determine from his answers whether his confusion was due to the knowledge that he was lost, or whether he was purposely deceiving us. The men all cried out that he was a traitor. On this he asked to be permitted to go some distance into a plain which was in full view, to try to make some discovery concerning the route. I told him he might go, but that I was suspicious of his conduct. From his first engagement he had claimed to know the way perfectly but now things looked different. I saw from the nature of the country that one who had once become acquainted with it could not forget it in a short time. I told him a few men would go with him to prevent his escape, and if he did not conduct us to the hunter's road he had frequently described as leading into Kaskaskia from the east I would have him immediately put to death. This I should have done, but after searching an hour or two he came to a place that he knew perfectly, and we now perceived that the poor fellow had been genuinely bewildered.

On the evening of July fourth we arrived within a few miles of the town, where we threw out scouts in advance and lay until nearly dark. We then resumed our march and took possession of a house on the bank of the Kaskaskia River, about three-quarters of a mile above the town, occupied by a large family. We learned from the inmates that the people had been under arms a few days before but had concluded the alarm to be groundless and at present all was quiet, and that there was a large number of men in town, although the Indians were for the most part absent. We obtained from the man boats enough to convey us across the river, where I formed my force in three divisions. I felt confident the inhabitants could not now obtain knowledge of our approach in time to enable them to make any resistance. My object was now to get possession of the place with as little confusion as possible, but to have it if necessary at the loss of the whole town. I did not entirely credit the information given us at the house, as the man seemed to contradict himself, informing us among other things that a noise we heard in the town was caused by the negroes at a dance. I set out for the fort with one division, ordering the other two to proceed to different quarters of the town. If I met with no resistance, at a certain signal a general shout was to be given and a certain part of the town was to be seized immediately, while men from each detachment who were able to talk French were to run through the streets proclaiming what had happened and informing the townsmen to remain in their houses on pain of being shot down.

These arrangements produced the desired effect, and within a very short time we were in complete possession of the place, with every avenue guarded to prevent any one from escaping and giving the alarm to the other villages. Various orders not worth mentioning had been issued for the guidance of the men in the event of opposition. Greater silence, I suppose, never reigned among the inhabitants of a town than in Kaskaskia at this juncture; not a person was to be seen or a word to be heard from them for some time. Meanwhile our troops purposely kept up the greatest possible noise throughout every quarter of the town, while patrols moved around it continually throughout the night, as it was a capital object to intercept any message that might be sent out. In about two hours all the inhabitants were disarmed, and informed that anyone who should be taken while attempting to escape from the place would immediately be put to death. Mr. Rochblave was secured, but some time elapsed before he could be gotten out of his room. I suppose he delayed to tell his wife what disposition to make of his public papers, but few of which were secured by us. Since his chamber was not entered during the night, she had ample opportunity to dispose of them, but how she did it we could never learn. I do not suppose she put them in her trunks, although we never examined them. From the idea she entertained of us she must have expected the loss even of her clothes.

During the night I sent for several individuals, from whom I sought to procure information, but obtained very little that was not already known to us. We learned, however, that the conduct of several of the inhabitants indicated them to be inclined to the American cause; that a large number of Indians were in the neighborhood of Cahokia; sixty miles distant; that Mr. Cerré,[28] a leading merchant and one of our most inveterate enemies, had left Kaskaskia with a large quantity of furs a few days before, enroute to Michilimackinac and thence to Quebec, from which place he had lately arrived at Kaskaskia; and that he was then in St. Louis, the Spanish capital, but his wife and family were still in town, together with a considerable quantity of goods which would be useful to our men.

In addition to Cerré, information was given me about numerous other individuals. I at once suspected that the object of the informers was to make their peace with me at the expense of their neighbors, and my situation demanded of me too much caution to permit giving them much satisfaction. I found Cerré to be one of the most eminent men of the country, with great influence over the people. I had some suspicion that his accusers were probably in debt to him, and hence desired to ruin him. What I had heard led me to feel that he was an object of importance to me, since he might

[28]Jean Gabriel Cerré was the most prominent merchant of British Illinois. A native of Canada, he came to Kaskaskia in 1755, and marrying there, made the Illinois country his future home. Clark describes for us how he was won over to the American cause. In 1779 Cerré removed to St. Louis, dying there in 1800. He was the father-in-law of Auguste Chouteau, one of the founders of that city, and famous in its early annals.

be wavering in his opinion respecting the merits of the war; and if he should take a decisive stand in our favor, he might prove a valuable acquisition. In short, his enemies led me to desire much to see him, and as he was then out of my power I had no doubt I could bring this about by means of his family who were in my hands. I immediately caused a guard to be stationed at his house and his stores to be sealed along with all the others. I did not doubt that when he should hear of this he would be extremely anxious for an interview.

By the morning of the fifth Messrs. Richard Winston[29] and Daniel Murray,[30] who proved to have been attached to the American cause, had plenty of provisions prepared. After the troops had regaled themselves they were with-

[29] Richard Winston was a Virginian who was trading in the western country at the close of the French and Indian War. He soon located at Kaskaskia, where upon the advent of Clark he promptly sided with the Americans and was appointed a captain by Clark. The following year he was made sheriff by John Todd, and when the latter left the Illinois Winston became deputy lieutenant-governor. He had much trouble in this position, and his devotion to the American cause brought about his financial ruin. He died in poverty in 1784, after having spent eighteen months at Richmond vainly prosecuting his claims before the Virginia government.

[30] Daniel Murray, like Winston, was a merchant at Kaskaskia, and like him gave the Americans important help. He remained in Kaskaskia during the following years and was finally shot in a quarrel over money matters.

drawn from the town and posted in extended position on its border. Every man had been expressly forbidden to hold any conversation with the inhabitants. All was distrust; their town was in complete possession of an enemy of whom they entertained the most horrid conception, and they were unable as yet to have any conversation with one of our people. Even those I talked with were ordered not to speak to any of my men. After some time they were told they could walk freely about the town. Finding they were busily engaged in conversation, I had a few of the principal militia officers put in irons, without hinting any reason or hearing anything they had to say in their own defense. The worst was now anticipated by all. I perceived the state of consternation the inhabitants were in, and in imagination, I suppose, felt all that they were experiencing in reality; and I felt perfectly disposed to act as arbiter between them and my duty.

After some time the priest[31] obtained permission to call on me, and came accompanied

[31] This was Father Pierre Gibault, a native of Canada, who came out to Illinois in the capacity of vicar-general in 1768. Locating at Kaskaskia, his parish included all the French settlements of the Illinois country and the Wabash. He threw his influence on the side of the Americans and rendered service of great importance to Clark in his conquest of the country. He was at Cahokia as late as 1791, but later withdrew to the Spanish side of the river and settled at New Madrid.

by five or six elderly gentlemen. However great the shock they had already sustained by reason of their situation, the addition when they entered the room where I was sitting with my officers was obvious and great. Having left our extra clothing at the Ohio River, we were almost naked; torn by the bushes and briers, we presented a dirty and savage aspect. So shocked were they that some time elapsed before they ventured to seat themselves, and still more before they would speak. At length we asked them what they wanted. The priest stated (after inquiring which of us was the commander) that as the townsmen expected to be separated, never, perhaps, to meet again, they had commissioned him to petition for permission to spend some time in the church taking their leave of each other. I knew that they supposed their very religion to be obnoxious to us. I carelessly told him, therefore, that I had nothing to say about his church and he might go there if he pleased; if he did, he was to tell the people not to leave the town. They attempted to introduce some other conversation, but were told that we were not at leisure; and, after answering a few questions, which I asked with a view to discouraging them from again coming to me with petitions, as they had not yet come to the state of mind I wanted, they went away. The whole populace now seemed to assemble in the church. The infants were carried along, and the houses were left for the most part without a person in them, with the exception of a few who cared little how things went and a few more who were not so much alarmed as the majority. I issued an order prohibiting the soldiers from entering the houses.

The people remained some time in the church, and, on breaking up, the priest and many of the principal citizens came to thank me for the indulgence shown them, and to beg permission to address me further on a subject dearer to them than all things else. They stated that their present situation was the fate of war and they were reconciled to the loss of their property; but they hoped I would not part them from their families, and that the women and children might keep some of their clothes and a small quantity of provisions, that they might support themselves by their industry. Their entire conduct had been influenced by their commandants, whom they had felt obliged to obey, and they were not much acquainted with the American war, as they had had but little opportunity to inform themselves. Many of them, however, had expressed themselves as strongly in favor of the Americans as they had dared. In short, they said everything that sensible men in their situation could be expected to advance, and their sole hope seemed to be to secure some lenity for their women and families, supposing their property would appease us. I felt convinced there was no finesse in all this, but that they really expressed their sentiments and the height of their expectations.

This was the point to which I had wished to bring them. I now asked them very abruptly whether they thought they were addressing savages. I told them that from the tenor of their conversation I was sure they did. Did they suppose we meant to strip the women and children or take the bread out of their mouths? Or that we would condescend to make war on women and children or the church? I informed them it was to prevent the effusion of innocent blood by the Indians, instigated thereto by their commandants and enemies, and not the prospect of plunder, that had caused us to visit them. As soon as this object was attained we would be perfectly satisfied; and as the king of France had joined the Americans (this information affected them very visibly) it was probable the war would shortly come to an end. They were at liberty to take whichever side they pleased without danger of losing their property or having their families distressed. As for their church, all religions would be tolerated in America, and so far were we from meddling with it, that any one who offered insult to it would be punished by me. To convince them we were not savages and plunderers, as they had conceived us to be, they might return to their families and tell them to conduct themselves as usual, with entire freedom and without any apprehension of danger.

I told them the information I had received since my arrival so fully convinced me that they had been influenced by false information given them by their leaders I was willing to forget all that had passed. Their friends who were in confinement would be released immediately and the guards withdrawn from every part of the town except the house of Cerré, and I only required compliance with a proclamation which I should immediately issue.

Such was the substance of my reply to them. They attempted to soften my idea that they had supposed us to be a set of savages and plunderers, or that they had supposed the property in a town belonged to those who captured it. I told them I knew they had been taught to believe that we were but little better than barbarians, but that we would say no more on the subject, and that I wished them to go and relieve the anxiety of the townsmen. Their feelings may more easily be imagined than expressed. They retired and in a few minutes the scene changed from an extreme state of dejection to one of great joy. Bells were rung, the church was crowded with people returning thanks, in short, every appearance of extravagant joy was manifested.

I immediately set about preparing a proclamation to be presented to them before they should leave the church, but wishing to test the people further, I postponed it for a few days. Feeling confident that any report that might now be sent out to the surrounding country would be favorable to us, I became more careless about who should go from or come into the town; but not knowing what might yet take place, I was uneasy over Cahokia and was determined as soon as possible to make a lodgement there and gain the place by some such stratagem as I had already employed at Kaskaskia.

I ordered Major Bowman to mount his company and part of another on horses to be procured from the town, and taking with him a few townsmen to inform their friends of what had happened, to proceed without delay to Cahokia and if possible gain possession of the place before the following morning. I gave him no further instructions on the subject, leaving him free to exercise his own judgment. He gave orders for collecting the horses, whereupon a number of gentlemen came to inform me that they were aware of the design. They pointed out that the soldiers were much fatigued, and said they hoped I would not reject their offer to execute whatever I might wish to have done at Cahokia. The people there were their friends and relatives and would, they thought, follow their example. At least, they hoped, they might be permitted to accompany the detachment.

Conceiving that it might be good policy to show them that we put confidence in them (which, in fact, I desired for obvious reasons to do), I told them I had no doubt Major Bowman would welcome their company and that as many as chose might go. Although we were too weak to be other than suspicious and much on our guard, I knew we had sufficient security for their good behavior. I told them that if they went at all they ought to go equipped for war. I was in hopes that everything would be settled amicably, but as it was the first time they had ever borne arms as freemen it might be well to equip themselves and see how they felt, especially as they were about to put their friends in the same situation as themselves.

They appeared to be highly pleased at this idea, and in the evening the Major set out with a force but little inferior to the one with which we had entered the country, the Frenchmen being commanded by their former militia officers. These new friends of ours were so elated over the thought of the parade they were to make at Cahokia that they were too much concerned about equipping themselves to appear to the best advantage. It was night before the party moved and the distance being twenty leagues, it was late in the morning of the sixth before they reached Cahokia. Detaining every person they met, they entered the outskirts of the town before they were discovered. The townsmen were at first much alarmed by this sudden appearance of strangers in hostile array and being ordered even by their friends and relatives to surrender the town. As the confusion among the women and children over the cry of the Big Knives being in town proved greater than had been anticipated, the Frenchmen immediately informed the people what had happened at Kaskaskia. Major Bowman told them not to be alarmed; that although resistance was out of the question he would convince them that he would prefer their friendship to their hostility. He was authorized to inform them that they were at liberty to become free Americans as their friends at Kaskaskia had done. Any who did not care to adopt this course were free to leave the country except such as had been engaged in inciting the Indians to war.

Cries of liberty and freedom, and huzzahs for the Americans rang through the whole town. The gentlemen from Kaskaskia dispersed among their friends and in a few hours all was amicably arranged, and Major Bowman snugly quartered in the old British fort. Some individuals said the town had been given up too tamely, but little attention was paid to them. A considerable number of Indians who were encamped in the neighborhood (Cahokia was an important center of Indian trade) immediately fled. One of the townsmen who was at St. Louis, some time later wrote a letter to me excusing himself for not paying me a visit. By July 8, Major Bowman had everything settled agreeably to our wishes. All of the inhabitants cheerfully took the oath of allegiance, and he set about repairing the fort and regulating the internal police of the place.

The neighboring villages followed the example set by Kaskaskia and Cahokia, and since we made no strict inquiry concerning those who had been engaged in encouraging the Indians to war, within a few days the country appeared to be in a state of perfect harmony. Friendly correspondence which was at once commenced between the Spanish officers and ourselves added much to the general tranquillity and happiness. It was not my fortune to enjoy pleasures of this kind. I found myself embarked on an enterprise that would require close attention and all the skill of which I was master to execute that service for my country which now appeared in prospect, with honor to it and with credit to myself.

Being now in position to procure all the information I desired, I was astonished at perceiving the pains and expense the British had incurred in inciting the Indians. They had sent emissaries to every tribe throughout that vast country, even bringing the denizens of Lake Superior by water to Detroit and there outfitting them for war. The sound of war was universal, there being scarcely a nation among them but what had declared and received the bloody belt and hatchet.

Vincennes I found to be a place of infinite importance for us to gain. This was now my object, but realizing that all the force we had, joined by every man in Kentucky, would not be able to take the place, I resolved on other measures than those of arms. I determined to send no message to the Indians for the present, but wishing an interview between us to be arranged through the agency of French gentlemen, to assume the appearance of carelessness about the matter. In all the papers I wrote I referred to myself as at the Falls of the Ohio, in order that it might appear that the troops we had with us were only a detachment from that place. I sought to spread the impression that the main body of our troops were fortifying that point, and that large reinforcements were daily expected, on the arrival of which we intended to continue the war. Every man we had was instructed to talk in this strain. Indeed, from many hints and pretended information of mine, before I left that place the greater part of them believed the most of this to be true. In short, as I had early perceived, an excuse for our marching into the Illinois country with so small a force was really necessary.

I inquired particularly into the manner the people had been governed heretofore and found, much to my satisfaction, that the government had generally been as severe as though under martial law. I resolved to make capital of this, and took every step in my power to cause the people to appreciate the blessings enjoyed by an American citizen. This enabled me, as I soon discovered, to support by their own choice almost supreme authority over them. I caused a court of civil judicature, elected by the people, to be established at Cahokia. Major Bowman, to the surprise of the people, held an election for a magistracy, and was himself elected judge of the court. His policy in holding an election can easily be perceived. After this similar courts were established at Kaskaskia and Vincennes. There was an appeal to myself in certain classes of cases, and I believe no people ever had their business done more to their satisfaction than these had for a considerable time by means of this regulation.

At the time of Major Bowman's arrival at Cahokia, Mr. Cerré, whom I have already mentioned, was still in St. Louis preparing to prosecute his journey to Canada. He was deterred from this in consequence of the news of our arrival. Agreeably to my expectation, upon learning the situation of affairs he resolved to return, but hearing that there was a guard kept at his house alone, and that several persons had attempted to ruin him with their information to me, he was advised not to cross the river without a safe-conduct. He applied to the Spanish governor for a letter requesting this, and coming to Ste. Genevieve, across the river from Kaskaskia, procured another of the same tenor from the commandant of that post and sent them both to me. However, all of the intercession he could arouse through the channel of Spanish officers and the solicitation of his particular friends, whom I found to constitute a great majority of the people, could not procure him a safe-conduct. I absolutely refused it, and intimated that I wished to hear no more on the subject; nor would I hear any person who had anything to say in vindication of him. I told them I understood Mr. Cerré to be a sensible man. If he were innocent of the allegations against him he would not be afraid to surrender himself. I added that his backwardness seemed to prove his guilt, and I felt very little concern about him.

I suppose rumor immediately carried this information to him, for in a few hours he crossed over the river and, without stopping to visit his family, presented himself before me. I told him that I supposed he was aware of the charges preferred against him, particularly that of inciting the Indians to murder, a crime that ought to be punished by all people who should be fortunate enough to get such culprits into their power; and that his recent backwardness about surrendering himself convinced me of his guilt. He replied that he was merely a merchant, that he never concerned himself about affairs of state further than the interest of his trade required, and that he had not as yet enjoyed opportunity to inform himself of the principles involved in the present contest sufficiently to enable him to form an opinion about it. He said he was so remote from the seat of war that he was doubtful of having heard more than one side of the question. He had learned more within the last few days than he had ever known before, and this information had only confirmed his former impression. I read to him part of a letter from Governor Hamilton[32] of Detroit to Mr. Rochblave, wherein he was alluded to in affectionate terms. He said that when he was at Detroit he behaved himself as became a subject, but he defied any man to prove that he had ever incited the Indians to war. Many people, on the contrary, had often heard him express his disapproval of the cruelty of such proceedings. He said there were several people in town who were

[32] Lieutenant-Governor Henry Hamilton of Detroit, Clark's antagonist in the Northwest, was of Irish birth and had served in the British army since 1754. He was appointed lieutenant-governor of Detroit in 1775, and assumed his new duties in November of that year. In the autumn of 1778 he advanced upon and captured Vincennes, only to be taken in turn, with his whole garrison, by Clark. Hamilton was much disliked by the Americans owing to their belief that he was active in stirring up Indian scalping parties against them. He was known to them as the "hair buying general." Clark sent him a prisoner to Virginia where he was closely confined and endured great hardship. On being exchanged in 1780 he visited England, returning to Canada as lieutenant-governor in 1782. He later served as governor of the Bermudas and of Dominica, dying at the latter place in 1796.

deeply indebted to him, and it might be the object of some of them to extricate themselves from their debts by ruining him. In his present situation it would be inconsistent for him to offer to declare his sentiments; but with respect to his part in the war he welcomed every investigation, as he had ever detested inciting the Indians. He sought to excuse his fears about coming across the Mississippi as soon as he could have wished.

Without making any further reply, I told him to withdraw into another room. The whole town was anxious to know his fate. I sent for his accusers, who were followed by a large number of townsmen, and had Mr. Cerré called in. I perceived plainly the confusion into which they were thrown by his appearance. I stated the case to the whole assembly, telling them that I never condemned a man unheard. I said that Cerré was now present and I was ready to do justice to the world in general by punishing him if he were found guilty of inciting to murder, or by acquitting him if he proved innocent of the charge. I closed by desiring them to submit their information.

Cerré undertook to speak to them but was ordered to desist. His accusers began to whisper among themselves and to retire for private conversation. At length only one out of six or seven was left in the room, and I asked him what he had to say to the point in question.

In short, I found that none of them had anything to say. I gave them a suitable reprimand and after some general conversation informed Mr. Cerré that I was happy to find he had so honorably acquitted himself of so black a charge. I told him he was now at liberty to dispose of himself and property as he pleased. If he chose to become a citizen of the United States it would give us pleasure. If he did not, he was at full liberty to do as he wished. He made many acknowledgments and concluded by saying that many doubts he had entertained were now cleared up to his satisfaction, and that he wished to take the oath of allegiance immediately. In short, he became a most valuable man to us. Simple as this transaction may appear, it had great weight with the people, and was of infinite service to us.

Everything in this section now wore a promising appearance, but Vincennes was never absent from my mind. I had reason to suspect from some things I had learned, that Mr. Gibault, the priest, had been inclined to the American interest previous to our arrival in the country. I had no doubt of his fidelity to us. Knowing he had great influence over the people, and that Vincennes was also under his jurisdiction, I sent for him and had a long conference on that subject. In response to my questions he stated that he did not think it worth my while to cause any military preparation to be made at the Falls for an attack on

Vincennes although the place was strong and there was a great number of Indians in the neighborhood. He said that Governor Abbott had left the place a few weeks since on some errand to Detroit. He thought that when the inhabitants should be fully informed of what had happened at the Illinois and the present happiness of their friends there, and should be fully acquainted with the nature of the war, their sentiments concerning it would undergo a great change. He was certain that his appearance there would have great weight even among the savages. If it were agreeable to me, he would take this matter upon himself, and he had no doubt of being able to bring the place over to the American interest without my being put to the trouble of marching troops against it. His business being altogether of a spiritual character, he desired that another person might be charged with the temporal part of the embassy, and named Dr. Laffont[33]

[33] We have only meager knowledge concerning Jean Baptiste Laffont, who proved so powerful an aid to the American cause at this juncture in Clark's affairs. He was a native of the West Indies, whence he removed to Florida and later to Kaskaskia, where we find him in the summer of 1770. He was still there in 1782, but by 1787 had removed to Vincennes. He died at Ste. Genevieve, probably about the year 1799. Prof. Alvord concludes (*Illinois Historical Collections* V, p. XXV-XXXII) that Laffont bore the main burden of the mission to Vincennes, in which Father Gibault aided with his influence, but for which he did not care to assume the responsibility.

as his associate, but he agreed that he would privately direct the whole undertaking.

This was quite in line with what I had been secretly aiming at for some days. The plan was immediately settled upon, and the two doctors with their intended retinue, among whom I placed a spy, set about preparing for their journey. On July 14 they set out with the following address,[34] taking with them, also, a large number of letters from their friends to the inhabitants at Vincennes. Dr. Laffont's instructions are now lost. I gave Mr. Gibault verbal instructions how to act in certain contingencies. It is mentioned here that Governor Abbott's letters to Mr. Rochblave had convinced us that the inhabitants were warmly attached to the American cause. This was wholly a piece of policy on my part. No such thing had been said; but as they would naturally suppose that Governor Abbott's letters to Rochblave had fallen into our hands, we knew that if they were led to suppose he had written in that style concerning them they would the more cordially verify it. Mr. Gibault had been led to believe this, and my authorizing them to garrison their own town would convince them of the great confidence we reposed in them. All this had its desired effect. Mr. Gibault and party arrived safely, and after spending a day or two in explaining matters to the people they universally acceded to the proposal (ex-

[34] Not included in the original manuscript.

cept for a few Europeans who had been left there by Mr. Abbott and who immediately left the country) and went in a body to the church, where the oath of allegiance was administered to them in the most solemn manner. A commander was elected and the fort was immediately taken possession of and the American flag displayed, to the great astonishment of the Indians.

Thus everything was settled beyond our most sanguine hopes. The people here at once assumed a new attitude; they began to talk in a different style and to act like perfect freemen. With a United States garrison at hand their language to the Indians was immediately altered; they informed the latter that their old Father, the King of France, had come to life again, and that he had joined the Big Knives and was angry at them for fighting for the English. They advised the Indians to make peace with the Americans as soon as possible; otherwise they might expect the land to be deluged with blood. Such was now the language the natives throughout that whole region received through correspondence from their ancient friends of the Wabash and the Illinois, and throughout all those tribes they began to reflect seriously upon it.

About the first of August, Mr. Gibault and party returned accompanied by several gentlemen of Vincennes, bringing the joyful news of our success at that place. His mission had caused me great anxiety, for without the possession of Vincennes all of our plans would have been blasted. During his absence I was exceedingly busy regulating matters in the Illinois towns. Our troops had been enlisted only for the period of time necessary to reduce these posts. I was now at a loss to decide upon my future course, and how far I might venture to stretch my authority, since, as it had been impossible to foresee the course of events, my instructions were silent on many important matters. To abandon the country and all the prospects open to us in the Indian department at this time for want of specific instructions in certain respects would, I thought, amount to a reflection on the government as having no confidence in me. I resolved, therefore, to assume all the authority necessary to carry out my designs.

I caused the greater part of my force to be reënlisted in a new military organization, and appointed French officers, residents of the country, to enroll a company of young Frenchmen. I established a garrison at Cahokia commanded by Captain Bowman, and another at Kaskaskia under Captain (formerly Lieutenant) Williams. Affairs at Vincennes remained in the situation I have already described. Colonel William Linn[35] who had accompanied us in the

[35] Prior to this Linn had performed one of the most brilliant exploits of the Revolution. In its early stage the colonists were in desperate need of powder. In

capacity of a volunteer, took charge of a party of men who were to be discharged on their arrival at the Falls and I sent orders for the removal of that post to the mainland. I dispatched Captain John Montgomery with letters to the seat of government in Virginia and to conduct thither, also, Mr. Rochblave.

The principles of this gentleman were so fixed and so violent against the United States that it was quite unsuitable to permit him to remain in the Illinois. His wife had taken

July, 1776, Linn and Captain George Gibson set out from Fort Pitt for distant New Orleans to obtain, if possible, a supply of powder from the Spanish commander there. They reached New Orleans in August and succeeded in procuring 10,000 pounds of powder. Gibson was thrown into prison by the Spanish, as a blind to lull the suspicions of the British consul, while Linn departed up river with the powder. He spent the winter at the Spanish post on the Arkansas, renewing his slow advance in the spring. Meanwhile Gibson, released from prison, made his way to Virginia carrying news of the issue of the enterprise, and the authorities there hastened to send a detachment to the relief of Linn. The latter, however, was beforehand with his plans, and by the first of May landed his precious cargo at Wheeling.

Linn was a native of New Jersey but grew up in western Maryland. He served in Forbes' army which captured Fort Duquesne in 1758. After Clark's Kaskaskia campaign Linn settled a station near Louisville. He served as colonel of militia in the Indian campaign of 1780. The following spring he was shot and killed by Indians near his home. He was an elder brother of Benjamin Linn, whom Clark sent out as a spy to Kaskaskia in 1777.

away all her furniture and other property; all but a few of her slaves were detained by us to be sold as plunder for the benefit of the soldiers. The sale did not take place for some time, as the officers generally wished the slaves to be returned to Mrs. Rochblave, and were in hopes that the men might be induced to agree to this. Many of them were men of sentiment, and the credit from such a course would be considerable, while the amount of money each would receive would be small. The desired result was in a fair way to take place, when some of the officers were requested to invite Mr. Rochblave (I had confined him to his room in order to protect him from the soldiers, as he seemed to take delight in insulting them at every opportunity and I was afraid that some of them might harm him) to spend the evening at a certain house with a number of his acquaintances. He accepted the invitation, but at the gathering he abused them in a most intolerable manner, calling them rebels and other similar names. They immediately sent him off to the guard house, and dismissed all further thought of saving his slaves. These were sold and the proceeds, amounting to about 1500 pounds, were divided among the men.

I informed the Governor, through Colonel Montgomery,[36] of all our proceedings and pres-

[36]Colonel Montgomery was a native and a prominent citizen of western Virginia who came to Kentucky in 1778 as one of Clark's four captains in his

ent prospects. I pointed out to him the necessity of immediately reinforcing us, and of sending some person to serve as head of the civil government, referring him to Captain Montgomery for full particulars. This party being dispatched, I turned my attention once more to Vincennes, and saw plainly that it was necessary to have an American officer at that post. Captain Leonard Helm appeared qualified to answer my purpose. He was past middle life, and was well acquainted with Indian affairs. I sent him to take command of that post, and also appointed him agent of Indian affairs for the department of the Wabash. I expected to receive reinforcements from the Governor by autumn, when a strong garrison should be sent to him. He was fully acquainted with my ideas and the plans I proposed to pursue, and about the middle of August set out to assume the duties of his new station.

An Indian chief, the son of Tobacco, a Piankeshaw at this place, lived in a village adjoining Vincennes. This man was called by the Indians the Grand Door to the Wabash, as the great Pontiac had been to the St. Joseph, since nothing of

Illinois campaign. When Clark retired to the Falls of Ohio after capturing Kaskaskia he left Montgomery in command of the Illinois country. At the close of the war he settled in Kentucky, removing later to Tennessee, where he founded Clarksville and named it in honor of his old commander. He was killed by Indians in 1794 near the mouth of the Cumberland River.

importance could be undertaken by the league on the Wabash without his consent. Perceiving that it was an object of great importance to win his support, I had sent him by Mr. Gibault a very complimentary message, and he had returned the compliment. I now sent him a message by Captain Helm calculated to influence him in the same fashion I had already done the townsmen. I also sent the following speech with a belt of wampum, and gave Captain Helm directions how to act, both if he should be pacifically inclined and in the contrary event. The Captain arrived safely at Vincennes, and was received with acclamation by the people. After the usual ceremonies were over, he sent for the Grand Door and delivered my letter to him. After reading it, the chief informed the Captain that he was happy to see him, one of the Big Knife chiefs, in this town. He admitted that he had joined with the English against the Americans, but confessed that he had always thought the sky looked gloomy. As the contents of the letter were a matter of great moment, he could not return an answer to it immediately, but must first hold a council on the subject, and he hoped the Captain would be patient. In short, he displayed all the courtly dignity he was master of, and Captain Helm followed his example. Several days elapsed before this business was concluded.

At length the Captain was invited to the Indian council, where he was informed by

Tobacco's son that they had carefully considered the case in hand, and the nature of the war between the English and ourselves had been explained to their satisfaction. He had always thought that he was in the dark as to the truth of the matter, but now the sky was clear. He perceived that the Big Knife was in the right, and observed that if the English should conquer us they would perhaps treat them in the same manner they intended to serve us. In short, his ideas were quite changed, and he would tell all the Indians of the Wabash to bloody the land no more for the English. At this he sprang up, struck his breast, called himself a man and a warrior, and saying that he was now a Big Knife, took Captain Helm by the hand. His example was followed by all present, and the evening was spent in merriment. Thus ended this important negotiation, which resulted in the saving of much blood. To the day of his death (which happened two years later) this man proved a zealous friend. In all his conduct he appeared to have the American interest much at heart. He desired to be buried near the Americans; his body was therefore conveyed to Cahokia and buried with the honors of war.

Within a short time almost all the tribes on the Wabash as far up as Ouiatanon came to Vincennes and followed the example of their head chief, and since expresses were continually passing back and forth between Captain

Helm and myself while these treaties were being arranged, everything was settled to my entire satisfaction and greatly to the public advantage. The British cause lost ground daily in this section, and in a short time our influence over the Indians extended to the River St. Joseph and the lower end of Lake Michigan. The French gentlemen at the different posts in our possession engaged themselves warmly in our cause. They appeared to vie with one another, by means of their correspondence and their trade among the Indians, in promoting our interest. In a short time large numbers of Indians belonging to tribes inhabiting the Illinois country, came to Cahokia to make peace with us. The information they obtained from the Frenchmen (whom they implicitly believed) concerning us greatly alarmed them, and we were visited by the greater part of them without any invitation on our part. This circumstance gave us a great advantage in that we could use with the greater propriety such language as suited our interest.

The treaties we made during the three or four weeks beginning about the last of August were negotiated in a different fashion, probably, than any others in America prior to that time. I had always been convinced that our general conduct of Indian affairs was wrong. Inviting them to treaties was considered by them in a different manner than we realized; they imputed it to fear on our part, and the giving of valuable presents confirmed them in this opinion. I resolved, therefore, to guard against this. I took great pains to acquaint myself with the French and Spanish methods of treating with the Indians, and with their disposition and manners in general. Since the Indians in this section had not been spoiled by us as yet, I made up my mind they should not be. I was fully prepared for the business, having copies at hand of the British treaties. After the ceremonies commonly employed at the commencement of Indian treaties, they, as the petitioning party, made the opening speech. They laid the entire blame for their taking up the bloody hatchet to the deception of the English, acknowledging their error and making many protestations that they would guard in future against those bad birds (alluding to the British emissaries sent among them) flying through the land. They concluded by expressing the hope that as the Great Spirit had brought us together for good, as He is good, they might be received as our friends, and that peace might take the place of the bloody belt, at the same time throwing down and stamping on the implements of war such as flags and red belts of wampum, which they had received from the British. I told them I had given attention to what they said, and that I would give them an answer the next day, when I hoped that the hearts and ears of all would be open to receive the truth, which should be pure without deception. I recommended that they keep themselves in readiness for the result of this day, on which their very existence as nations perhaps depended. I then dismissed them, not suffering any of our people to shake hands with them, as peace was not yet concluded. I told them it was time enough to give the hand when the heart could be given also. They replied that such sentiments were those of men who had but one heart, and who did not speak with a double tongue.

On the following day I delivered this speech:

Men and warriors, pay attention. You informed me yesterday that the Great Spirit had brought us together, which you hoped was good, as He is good. I also have the same hope, and whatever may be agreed upon by us at the present time, whether for peace or war, I expect each party will strictly adhere to and henceforward prove ourselves worthy of the attention of the Great Spirit. I am a man and a warrior, not a councillor. I carry War in my right hand and in my left Peace. I was sent by the great council fire of the Big Knives and their friends to take control of all the towns the English possess in this country, and to remain here watching the conduct of the red men. I was sent to bloody the paths of those who continue the effort to stop the course of the rivers, but to clear the roads that lead from us to those who wish to be in friendship with us, in order that the women and children may walk in them without anything being in the way to strike their feet against; and to continue to call on the Great Fire for warriors enough to darken the land of those who are hostile to us, so that the inhabitants shall hear no sound in it but that of birds that live on blood. I know that a mist is yet before your eyes; I will dispel the clouds in order that you may see clearly the cause of the war between the Big Knives and the English, that you may judge for yourselves which is in the right. Then if you are men and warriors, as you profess to be, prove it by adhering strictly to what you may now declare, without deceiving either party, and thus proving yourselves to be only old women.

The Big Knives are very much like the red men; they do not know well how to make blankets, powder, and cloth; they buy these things from the English (from whom they formerly descended) and live chiefly by raising corn, hunting, and trading, as you and your neighbors, the French do. But the Big Knives were daily becoming more numerous, like the trees in the woods, so that the land became poor and the hunting scarce; and having but little to trade with, the women began to cry to see their children naked, and tried to make clothes for themselves, and soon gave their husbands blankets of their own making; and the men learned to make guns and powder, so that they did not want so much from the English. Then the English became angry and stationed strong garrisons through all our country (as you see they have done among you on the lakes and among the French) and would not let our women spin nor the men make powder, nor let us trade with anybody else. They said we must buy everything from them, and since we had become saucy they would make us give them two bucks for a blanket that we used to get for one. They said we must do as they pleased, and they killed some of us to make the rest afraid. This is the truth and the cause of the war between us, which did not begin until some time after they had treated us in this fashion. Our women and children were cold and hungry, and continued to cry. Our young men were lost, and there were no counsellors to set them in the right path. The whole land was dark, and the old men hung down their heads for shame, for they could not see the sun.

Thus there was mourning for many years. At last the Great Spirit took pity on us and kindled a great council fire that never goes out, at a place called Philadelphia. He stuck down a post there and left a war tomahawk by it, and went away. The sun at once broke out, and the sky became blue. The old men held up their heads, and assembled at the fire. They sharpened the hatchet and put it into the hands of the young men, and told them to strike the English as long as they could find one on this side of the Great Water. The young men immediately struck the war post and blood ensued. Thus the war began, and the English were driven from one place to another, until they became weak and hired you red men to fight for them, and help them. The Great Spirit became angry at this, and caused your Old Father, the French king, and other great nations to join the Big Knives and fight with them against all their enemies, so that the English have become like a deer in the woods. From this you may see that it is the Great Spirit that caused your waters to be troubled, because you fought for the people he was angry with, and if your women and children should cry you must blame yourselves for it, and not the Big Knives.

You can now judge who is in the right. I have already told you who I am. Here is a bloody belt and a white one. Take whichever you please. Behave like men, and don't let your present situation, being surrounded by the Big Knives, cause you to take up the one belt with your hands when your hearts drink up the other. If you take the bloody path you shall go from this town in safety and join your friends, the English, and we will try like warriors who can put the most stumbling blocks in the road and keep our clothes perfumed with blood the longest. If you should take the path of peace and now be received as brothers to the Big Knives and the French, and should hereafter listen to bad birds that will be flying through your land, you will no longer be counted as men but as persons with two tongues, who ought to be destroyed without listening to what you say, as nobody could understand you. Since I am convinced that you have never heard the truth before, I do not wish you to give me an answer before you have had time to council if you wish to do this. We will part this evening and when you are ready, if the Great Spirit will bring us together again, let us prove ourselves worthy by speaking and thinking with but one heart and one tongue.

What their private consultations upon this speech were, we never could learn, but on their return the next day, the business commenced with more than usual ceremony. A new fire was kindled, all the gentlemen of the town were collected, and after all their preparatory ceremonies were through, the chief who was to speak advanced to the table where I sat, with the belt of peace in his hand; another with the sacred pipe, and a third with the fire to kindle it. The pipe was first presented to the heavens then to the earth, and completing the circle it was then presented to all the spirits, invoking them to witness what was about to be concluded, then to myself and, descending in order, to every person present.

The speaker then addressed himself to the Indians. The substance of his talk was that they ought to be thankful that the Great Spirit had taken pity on them, and had cleared the sky and opened their ears and hearts so that they could hear and receive the truth. Addressing himself to me, he said they had paid great attention to what the Great Spirit had put into my heart to say to them. They believed that it was all true, since the Big Knives did not speak like any other people they had ever heard. They now saw plainly that they had been deceived by the English, who had told them lies and never the truth. This, some of their old men had always said, and now they believed it. They said that we were in the right, and as the English had forts in their country, they might, if they became strong, want to serve the red people as they did the Big Knives; and that they, the red men, ought to help us. They had taken up the belt of peace with a sincere heart, and spurned the other away. They were determined to hold it fast, and would have no doubt of our friendship, as they saw from our manner of speaking that there was no room for suspicion. They would call in all their warriors, and cast the tomahawk into the river where it could never be found again. They would suffer no more emissaries or bad birds to pass through their land to disquiet their women and children, that they might always be cheerful to smooth the roads for their brothers the Big Knives whenever they should come to see them. They said they would send word to all their friends, letting them know what had been done and the good talk they had heard, and would advise them to listen to it. They hoped I would send men among them to see for myself that they were men and that they adhered strictly to all that had been said at this great fire which the Great Spirit had kindled here at Cahokia for the good of all who would listen to it.

This is the substance of their answer to me. The pipe was again kindled and presented to all the spirits to be witnesses, and with smoking and shaking of hands this grand piece of business was concluded, with as much dignity and importance in their eyes, I suppose, as was the treaty between France and America in ours. The Indians now assumed a different attitude. Close harmony reigned without any appearance of distrust on their side, but we were not quite so complaisant. I had resolved never to do anything that should have the appearance of courting them, and I generally made some excuse for the little I presented, such as, having come a long way to see me, they had expended their ammunition, worn out their leggings, or met with some misfortune or other. But they were genuinely alarmed; the conclusion of peace satisfied them, and they parted from us with every appearance of perfect satisfaction. I consistently made it a point to keep spies out among them, and was pleased to find that the great majority of those who treated with us adhered strictly to their agreement, so that before long we could send a single soldier through any part of the Wabash and Illinois country, for in the course of this fall all the Indians of these regions came to treat with us, either at Cahokia or Vincennes.

It is not worth while dwelling on the particulars of every treaty. The one already mentioned conveys an idea of the plan we adopted. All negotiations were carried out in accordance with the same principles, always sticking to the text, but varying with the different tribes in the manner of delivery. Sometimes we were more severe, but never more lenient, although a very different kind of language was employed, of course, toward those with whom we were on terms of friendship. Their replies were nearly the same throughout all the tribes, and a boundary between the British emissaries and our own appeared now to be fixed at the heads of the waters of the Great Lakes and those of the Mississippi. Since neither party cared to venture too far, some of the tribes became divided among themselves, part siding with us, and part with the English. So sudden a change in our favor among the Indians in this region required great attention to keep the flame from cooling too soon, as the appearance of a reinforcement which we had reason to expect in the autumn would renew our influence. Every method was employed to convince the French inhabitants that their interests were being studied by us. Every disagreeable restriction that they had formerly been subject to was done away with, and business with the commanding officers was conducted without ceremony, nor was there any ceremony about the courts, which held weekly sessions. These things and many other minor ones produced a good effect; through them our cause was considerably promoted among their friends on the lakes and many traders, watching their opportunity, came over with their goods and settled in the Illinois country and at Vincennes. This had a good effect upon the Indians. The friendly correspondence between the Spaniards and ourselves was also much to our advantage, since everything the Indians heard from them was favorable to us.

The behavior of two young men at the time of these treaties at Cahokia affected me deeply, and the relation of their conduct may perhaps not be disagreeable to you. A party known as the Meadow Indians, that roved about among the different nations, being composed of stragglers from all of them, were informed that if they would contrive to make me prisoner, they would receive a great reward. With this design they came down to Cahokia as others had done, pretending to treat for peace. Pretending some acquaintance with Mr. Brady, they were lodged in his yard, about one hundred yards from my quarters and nearly the same distance from the fort. The little river Cahokia, which was there about knee-deep, fronted the house on the opposite side of the street. Having business at times with the other Indians, they loitered about, listened to what was passing, and became pretty well acquainted with our people. I had received but a bad report of them, and took but little apparent notice of them. Observing that the house I lodged in was very quiet by night, and supposing it had but few guards, they formed their plan in the following manner: Some of them were to cross the river and fire off their guns opposite their camping quarters, upon which they were to attempt to gain the protection of the guard on the pretence of flying from hostile Indians who had fired on them from across the river. If they succeeded, they were to butcher the guard and carry me off.

A few nights after their arrival they made the attempt, about one o'clock. Having too many things to think about to sleep much, I happened to be awake at the time the alarm was given. They were immediately at the gate when the sentinel presented his piece. The night being light, they saw the guard parading before the door more numerous than they had expected, and taking a by-way they returned to their quarters. The whole town was now under arms. The guard was positive it was these Indians, and they were immediately examined. They said that their enemies had fired on them across the creek; that they wanted to get under the protection of the guard but were not permitted to do so, and so made the best of their way back to defend themselves. Some of the French gentlemen, however, being better acquainted with them than the rest of us, insisted it was they that had given the alarm; and sending for a candle discovered that the leggings and moccasins of those who had crossed the river were quite wet and muddy. They were quite confounded at this. They sought to make various excuses, but their design was easily seen through, and they were not suffered to speak. I said but little to them, and as there were many Indians of other nations in town, to convince the whole of the strict union between the French and ourselves, I told them that as they had disturbed the town the people might do what they pleased with them, and went away, whispering, however, that the chiefs should be sent to the guardhouse and put in irons, which was immediately done by the inhabitants. In this situation they were brought every day into the council, but not sufferred to speak. When I had finished with the others I had their irons taken off and told them their design was obvious to me, as a bird from their country had whispered in my ear; that everyone said they ought to die, which was what I had intended and which they must themselves see they deserved; but that on considering the matter and the meanness of the attempt to watch and catch a bear asleep, I found that you were only old women and too mean to be killed by a Big Knife. But as you ought to be punished for putting on breech-cloths like men, these shall be taken away from you, and plenty of provisions given you to go home, as women don't know how to hunt; and as long at you stay here you shall be treated as all squaws ought to be.

Without taking any further notice of them, I proceeded to converse indifferently with others present on various trifling subjects. They appeared to be much agitated. After some time they rose and advanced with a belt and pipes of peace, which they presented to me and made a speech which I would not suffer to be interpreted to me at that time. Laying my sword on the table, I broke their pipe and told them that the Big Knives never treated with women, and for them to sit down and enjoy themselves as others did and not be afraid. The substance of their speech was an acknowledgment of their design, which they excused by saying some bad men from Mackinac had put it into their heads. They hoped we would take pity on their women and children, and as their lives had been spared when they deserved to lose them, they were in hopes that peace would be granted them as it was to other tribes.

Several chiefs of other tribes present spoke in their favor, condemning their attempt. They said that they saw the Big Knife was above little things, and they were confident I would take pity on the families of these men and grant them peace. I told them that I had never made war upon them. If the Big Knives came across such people in the woods, they commonly shot them down as they did wolves, to prevent their eating the deer, but they never talked about it. The conversation on the subject ceased, and for some time these fellows continued busily engaged in private conversation. At length two young men advanced to the middle of the floor, sat down, and flung their blankets over their heads. At first I did not know what to make of this action; however, two of the chiefs with a (peace) pipe stationed themselves by them, and delivered speeches in much the same manner as they had previously done, concluding by saying they offered these two young men as an atonement for their guilt and hoped that the Big Knives would be reconciled by this sacrifice of their people. They again offered me the pipe, which I refused, telling them, but in a milder tone than I had previously employed, to sit down and that I would have nothing to say to them. It appeared that these people had become so thoroughly alarmed that they supposed a tomahawk was hanging over the head of every one of their nation. They thought nothing would save them but to secure peace before they left the place; and they supposed that by putting to death these two young men, or keeping them as slaves, we would become reconciled with them.

The young men retained their first position, frequently pushing the blanket aside as if impatient to know their fate. I had no expectation of this business ending in this manner. I had intended all along to let myself be finally persuaded to grant peace to these people, but this action on their part astonished me. I hardly knew whether or not it was sincere, although everything indicated that it was. Every person of the large gathering present appeared anxious to know what would be done, and a general silence fell upon them and for some time all were in a state of suspense.

You may easily guess my feelings on this occasion and the pleasure with which I regarded these young men. I had read of some such action as this, but had never known whether or not to credit it. Never before nor since have I felt so capable of speaking. I ordered the young men to rise and uncover themselves. Upon this there was a very visible alteration in their countenances, which, however, they appeared to try to conceal. I harangued the whole assembly in suitable fashion on the subject, concluding by telling them I was happy to find there were men among all nations, as we were now witnesses to the fact that there were at least two among these people. I then addressed the young men, praising them much and concluding by saying it was only with men such as they as chiefs of a nation that I cared to treat; and that through them the Big

Knife granted peace and friendship to their people. I took them by the hand as my brothers and chiefs of their nation and said I expected all present to acknowledge them as such. I presented them first to my own officers, then to the French and Spanish gentlemen present, and lastly to the Indians, all of whom greeted them as chiefs. I concluded the business by having them saluted by the garrison. I wish I had a copy or could remember all that was said on this occasion, but you may easily conceive what was said from the character of the affair. It appeared to give general satisfaction, but I thought the old chiefs appeared to be much cowed. Our new nabobs were now treated with great respect on all occasions. A council was called in order to do some business with them, and great ceremony was employed in order to rivet more firmly what had been done. On their departure I gave them some presents to distribute among their friends at home, by whom I understood they were acknowledged as chiefs and held in great esteem, and that the Americans were much spoken of among them.

It would be difficult to overestimate the consequences which would have ensued had they succeeded in their plan. However badly it may appear, to have been devised, it was the most probable one open to them. They could not have attempted to carry out their project in town in the daytime, and I never went out of it without too strong a guard for them to overcome. As it turned out, the affair proved a fortunate one for us. It gained us much credit and had a good effect upon the Indians in the quarter, as it soon became a subject of general conversation among them.

I now turned my attention to Saguina, Mr. Blackbird, and Nakewoin, two chiefs of the bands of Sauteur and Ottawa tribes bordering on Lake Michigan and the river St. Joseph. Mr. Blackbird and party were at St. Louis at the time Major Bowman took possession of Cahokia. Knowing that their tribe was warmly engaged in the war, and not believing the Spanish protection sufficient to secure them against the revenge of the Big Knives who were so near at hand, although the governor assured them of the certainty of their being kindly received, they became alarmed and pushed off. On their passage up the Illinois river these chiefs met with a number of traders who had heard what had taken place among their friends in the Illinois and had already begun to alter their tone toward the Indians, persuading Blackbird to turn back and call upon the Big Knives, saying that as he had been so near them and did not go to see them they would think that he had run away through fear. He excused himself by saying his family was sick, but that he would go in the spring and meantime would write us a letter. I suppose he thought this would lead us to believe they were our friends, and I have no doubt but that their sentiments daily changed in our favor. I made strict inquiry about Blackbird and Nakewoin. I found that they were chiefs of considerable St. Joseph's river bands who were then at war with us, and that Blackbird had great influence in that quarter. Some traders recently arrived at the Illinois thought he really wanted a conference with us but held back awaiting an invitation. I gave a man who satisfied my purpose $200 to visit Blackbird at the St. Joseph river and sent him a full answer to his letter, inviting him to come to Kaskaskia in the fall. This he did with only eight attendants, aside from my messenger, Denoe. After they had rested and refreshed themselves, observing some of the usual preparations being made for an Indian council, Blackbird sent word to me that he had come to see me on business of consequence to both our nations, and wished that we should not spend our time in ceremony. He said it was customary among all Indians but it was not necessary between us and that we could do our business much better sitting at a table. He desired to have a long talk with me, and hoped there would be no ceremony employed. I perceived that Mr. Blackbird conducted matters differently than other chiefs, and that he assumed the airs of a polite gentleman. Accordingly a room was prepared and the nabob was formally introduced to me by a French gentleman. After the exchange of a few compliments he took a seat at the end of the table opposite me, with the interpreters at our right and left, and the gentlemen seated round the room. Blackbird opened the discussion and attempted to speak as much in the European fashion as possible. He said that he had long desired to have some conversation with the chief of our nation, but had never before enjoyed the opportunity to do so. He had conversed with prisoners, but he placed little confidence in what they said as they were generally afraid to talk. He said he had been engaged in the war for some time, but had always doubted the propriety of it, as the English and the Americans appeared to be the same people. He was sensible that there was some mystery with which he was unacquainted. He had heard only one side of the story, and now wished me to explain it fully to him in order that, having heard both sides, he might be in a position to judge for himself.

To satisfy this inquisitive Indian I was obliged to begin almost at the first settlement of America and go through its entire history to the present time, dwelling particularly on the cause of the Revolution; and since I could not speak to him in similes as I did to other Indians, it took me nearly half a day to satisfy him. He asked a large number of very pertinent questions and required to be satisfied upon every point. I was the better able to satisfy him as I was now pretty well acquainted with all that the British officers had told the Indians.

Blackbird appeared to be quite satisfied and said he was convinced from many circumstances that I had given a true account of the matter. He had long suspected from the conduct of the English that they wished to keep the Indians in the dark and it was now very obvious to him. He thought the Americans were quite right and that they ought to be assisted rather than opposed. He was happy to find that their old friends, the French, had joined us, and said the Indians ought to do likewise, but as I had said we did not wish this they ought at least to remain neutral. He said he would not blame us if we drove all that would not do so off the face of the earth. It was plain to him that the English were afraid; otherwise they would not give so many goods to the Indians to fight for them. He himself was perfectly satisfied about the matter, and I might rest assured that his sentiments were fixed in our favor and that he would no longer pay any attention to the English. He said that he would immediately bring the war to an end as far as his part was concerned. As many of their young men were then out on the warpath, however, I must excuse this, but as soon as they returned he would make them lay down their arms and no one whom he could influence should take them up again. Upon his return home he would take pains to tell the Indians of every denomination what had passed between us, and would inform them of the true cause of the war. He felt sure that most of them would follow his example, but it would have a good effect if I would send a young man among them under his protection (which I did), as his appearance would give great weight to what he himself might say to them. He hoped that for the future we would look upon each other as friends and that a correspondence should be kept up between us.

I told him I was happy to find that our business was likely to end so much to our mutual satisfaction, and to the advantage and tranquility of our respective nations. I promised immediately to inform the Governor of Virginia of what had passed between us, and said I knew it would give all the American people great pleasure, and that he (Blackbird) would be regarded among their friends. After spending a few days with us he returned home, accompanied by a young man who went as my agent. I had two pack horses loaded with necessary supplies for Blackbird's return journey and sent some presents to his family, to the amount, perhaps, of $20 or $30. Thus ended the negotiation between this chief and myself, and as I had frequent opportunity of hearing from him in the course of the fall I found that he adhered strictly to what he had promised me. He not only withdrew his own tribe from the war, but caused great numbers of Indians in that quarter to become very cold toward the British interest.

I thought it policy in the course of all my conversations with the Indians to tell them I did not blame them for accepting the presents that the British chose to give them, but that it was degrading to them to make war as hirelings. I said that this was beneath the dignity of a warrior, and that the Big Knives regarded those that were at war against them on their own account with more respect than they did the hireling. I said the scalps of the one were kept by us as great trophies, while those of the other were given to the children to play with or thrown to the dogs. The employment of such language to a people with whom we ardently wished to be at peace may appear strange, but it produced a good effect among people of their education and was perfectly consonant with our policy.

About this time I received a letter from a chief named Lajes or the Big Gate. It seems that at the time Pontiac besieged Detroit this fellow, then a lad, had shot a man standing at a gate and immediately the name of Big Gate was given to him as a mark of honor. He had early engaged in the British interest, and had led several war parties against our frontiers with good success. On hearing what was going on in the Illinois country, he fell in with some Potawatomi who were on their way to visit us and came with them to hear what we had to say for ourselves. He had the assurance to make his appearance before me in a complete war dress, and with the bloody belt he had received from the English hanging round his neck. He attended the councils for several days, always placing himself at the front of the room and sitting in great state, without saying a word to us or we to him. I had found out what I wanted to know about him and had fixed upon my course of action, and during my business with the other Indians I had employed several speeches designed to prepare my associates for what was coming. On the conclusion of our business I addressed myself to him, telling him that I had been informed who he was but as he knew public business must be attended to before private ceremonies, I hoped he would excuse my not having spoken to him sooner. I said it was customary among white people that when officers met in this manner, even though they were enemies, they treated each other with greater respect than they did common people, and esteemed each other the more in proportion to the exploits each had performed against the other's nation. As he had come designedly to see us and our business was now over, I hoped he would spend a few days more with us and that he would do us the pleasure of dining with the Big Knife that evening.

He appeared to be on nettles and, rising, began to excuse himself. I would not listen, but ran on upon the same theme. I would stop, he would commence, and I would begin again, until I found I had worked him up to as high a pitch as I desired and then permitted him to go on. He stepped to the middle of the room and removed his war belt and a small British flag from his bosom, flung them on the floor, followed by all of his clothing except his breech-cloth, then, striking his breast, he addressed the entire audience, telling them they knew he had been a warrior from his youth. He said he delighted in war, but that the English had told him lies. He thought from what they said that the Big Knives were in the wrong. He had been to war against them three times, and was ready to go again, but concluded he would rest himself for a while and come and see what sort of people they were, and hear how they talked. He had listened to everything that had been said and was now convinced that the English were wrong and the Big Knives right. He said that as a man and warrior he would not fight in a wrong cause; that he had flung away the bloody clothes the English had given him, and giving them a kick across the room he struck his breast and, saying that he was now a Big Knife, came and shook hands with me and the whole company, as his brothers. A great deal of merriment ensued.

The whole company appeared diverted, and the Big Gate being a merry fellow himself, kept up their good humor by speaking to them as a new man and a Big Knife. But as our new brother was now naked, it was necessary that he should be clothed. The things he had pulled off were pushed into the street as despised, by one of the servants, and Captain McCarty[37] having presented him with a suit covered with lace, at dinner Captain Big Gate was much the finest man at the table. In order to appear in as much state as the rest of us, he had ordered one of his men to wait on him. This was rather awkward, as we had suffered none of the Indians to dine with us except chiefs of the greatest dignity. Pains were taken to prevent any jealousy on the part of those in town who were of as high rank as Mr. Lajes.

After dinner was over he told me he wished to have some private conversation with me, and pointed to a room that had a large window opening into a back street. Being always suspicious, I did not know whether my new brother intended to stab me and make his escape through the window. I took precautions against this without his knowing it, and we were shut up with the interpreter nearly half

[37] Captain Richard McCarty was a trader from Canada who had located at Cahokia. He joined the American cause and was made commandant here in 1779, in which position he became involved in conflict with the civil authorities. In the summer of 1781 he was killed by Indians while enroute to Virginia to lay before the authorities a complaint of the inhabitants of Kaskaskia against certain of the American officials.

an hour. He gave me a history of himself and a full account of the situation of affairs at Detroit. He said he could do almost anything he pleased at that place. If I desired it he would go and bring me a scalp or a prisoner within forty days, since they did not know what had happened here and he would have the opportunity to do what he pleased. I told him we never wanted the Indians to fight for us. All we wished of them was to sit still and look on. Those who did not do this might expect to be swallowed up as they would see the lakes covered with boats belonging to the Big Knives. I desired him on no account to kill any person on our behalf. I told him I would be glad to have him bring me news or a prisoner if he could readily obtain one, but by no means to injure him, as it was beneath our principles to treat prisoners ill.

I presented him with a medal and a captain's commission. On the day he took his departure, with many Indians accompanying him he came to take his leave of me at my quarters. There were many gentlemen present and they saluted him by firing their pistols through the window, and on passing in front of them he was again saluted. This elated him greatly. He had not gone far before he stopped, and saying he supposed those poor soldiers were hungry for a dram, he ordered one of his men to go to a trader with whom he was acquainted and who was then in town, and get a little keg of rum and give it to them to drink his health. When this was done he went away by water up the Illinois river. Here he fell in with some traders of his acquaintance who had obtained a permit at Mackinac to trade in this section, and were then on their way to us. Lajes asked them which way they were going. They said they were only trading. He then asked them if they were not afraid of the Big Knives at Cahokia. They said they were not. He then inquired whom they were for, and they asked him what he meant by this. He answered, "Are you for the King of England or the Big Knives?" Knowing the fellow's character, they said certainly they were for the King of England, and asked if he was not also for him. He said no, he was a captain of the Big Knives, and producing his commission told them they were enemies to his country and his prisoners, and that he would return them to his superior officer at Cahokia.

The men became alarmed, not knowing what to make of the fellow, but they found he was in earnest and he had a commission under my hand and seal. They then told him they were running away and were going to the Big Knives. He said they were liars and he would not believe them. He pestered them for two or three days until a party came along whom he knew to be in the American interest and became surety that they would deliver themselves up to me, and had a letter, which he dictated, written to me. He warned the men to take care of themselves, for if they proved deceitful and fell into his hands again he would treat them ill. This was a curious Indian letter. I can't remember the particulars of it further than that it pertained to the foregoing matter. It is lost with all the papers of this year except a few that I have by chance recovered.

Captain Big Gate proceeded on his journey, and as long as I knew of him continued to behave well, speaking much of his new dignities and abusing the other Indians for fighting as hirelings, and so forth. Whether or not he ever afterward joined the British I never learned.

By this time we had done business with almost all the Indians of the Wabash and the Illinois as far up as the Iowa and the Sauk and Reynards, and those living at the lower end of Lake Michigan, and the country appeared at this time to be in a state of perfect tranquility. I was pleased to learn that our new post at the falls of the Ohio continued to gather strength, as also Kentucky in general; and that a powerful expedition was to move from Pittsburgh upon Detroit. This information, with the thought of what we had already done, caused us to enjoy ourselves for the first time since our arrival. Our joy, however, did not last long.

Some Indians from the Missouri came from several hundred miles up that river to see us. Their curiosity was so great they could not resist the temptation. They told us their business was merely to pay us a visit. They said they had often heard of the Big Knives and wished to see them and hoped that their curiosity might be excused. We granted their request and treated them kindly while they were with us. They were somewhat different in their manner and complexion, being much fairer than any other Indians I had ever seen. I suppose it was this that gave rise to the idea of there being Welsh Indians in that quarter.[38]

Captain Helm sent an express to inform me that the British had sent an agent to Ouiatanon with a considerable supply of goods to attempt to regain the affections of the Indians in that quarter. He said he thought the man might be taken if I would authorize the attempt, and that several gentlemen at Vincennes shared

[38] There is a tradition that one Madoc, a Welsh prince of the twelfth century, disgusted at the dissensions which prevailed in his native land, resolved to explore the western ocean in search of more tranquil scenes. He came to America with a numerous company, and their descendants, mingling with the natives, were the so-called "Welsh Indians." The belief in their existence has been very persistent, and many of the older writers on American history discuss the subject. George Catlin, the noted student and artist of Indian life, identified the Mandan Indians of the upper Missouri as the Welsh Indians. A full discussion of the subject with citations from many authorities may be found in Reuben T. Durrett's *Traditions of the Earliest Visits of Foreigners to North America* (Louisville, 1908. Filson Club Publications, No. 23).

this opinion. I gave my approval of the enterprise and authorized the Captain to act in accordance with the decisions of the councils they might hold; but I told him that if they at any time should find the enterprise dangerous or the chances against them, to relinquish it and return, giving out word that they had merely made a small excursion to see their friends. He set out up the Wabash by water with men, chiefly inhabitants of Vincennes. The French merchants with the expedition traded with the Indians along the way, and Captain Helm addressed them on public affairs; this was to give the impression that he was merely paying a visit to them, and that the Frenchmen with him had come along to look after their trade. The party did not display any hostile intention until it reached the vicinity of the Wea town. They then made all possible speed, and entering the fort took prisoner The Kite and twenty or thirty Chippewa warriors who were in council there. The British agent (I forget his name) heard frequently of the advance of this party up the river, but he was told by the Indians they intended no harm. They said that the Big Knife who was with the party merely came along with the traders to deliver good talks to his friends, and so forth. But after a few days the agent began to suspect the sincerity of the Indians and retired up the river a short time before Captain Helm arrived.

Those Chippewas were a party which he had invited to meet at Ouiatanon to get supplies and conduct an expedition against Vincennes. They arrived but a few minutes before our party. Hearing the news and finding their friends gone they slipped into the fort to take some refreshments and hold a council. This they had scarcely begun when our party entered and closed the gate on them. As the inhabitants did not give them notice of its approach the Indians were much alarmed at finding themselves so suddenly captured and at first had little to say for themselves. After some consultation between Captain Helm and the French gentlemen who were with him it was thought that capital might be made of this adventure and accordingly a plan was fixed upon. A great deal was said to the prisoners, but it all amounted to this: that the Big Knives disdained to catch a prisoner asleep, and since that was the case in the present instance the Indians were at liberty and might fight for the English as long as they pleased; but if they should again fall into the hands of the Big Knives they need expect no mercy. The Indians gave suitable answer to this act of seeming generosity, declaring that they would never fight against the Big Knives again; and I understood that the Indians frequently mentioned this adventure and spoke much in our favor. Our party returned in safety to Vincennes, having spoken with the greater part of the Indians to the apparent satisfaction of both parties. So great was our influence among the Indians at this period that Governor Hamilton on his expedition against Vincennes with all his influence could raise but four or five hundred Indians to accompany him.

The Chickasaws being at war I wished to have some correspondence with them in order to learn their sentiments. I did not care to send to them, however, since this would appear too much like begging a peace as they call it. It occurred to me that the Kaskaskia Indians had long been at war with the Chickasaws; for some time this war had seemingly subsided, and Batisst, the chief of the Kaskaskias, I knew was strongly disposed in our favor. I therefore suggested that he should go and propose a firm peace with the Chickasaws, and if he succeeded should mention something about the Big Knives. I was in hopes in this way to bring about a correspondence with them. Batisst went without being apprised of my real design. The Chickasaws received him cordially, but he could not conclude his business on account of the absence of some of the chiefs. He mentioned the Americans, but their conversation on the subject was cool and little was accomplished.

Winter was now approaching, and affairs began to wear a more gloomy aspect. I had not as yet received word from the authorities in Virginia. On the other hand I learned from various sources that preparations were under way at Detroit for a great expedition; an advance had already been made as far as the Miami town and talks had been sent to all the Indian tribes. We supposed that these preparations were designed to the end of giving the army from Fort Pitt as warm a reception as possible. This information gave us much pleasure until we learned that instead of marching into Detroit the army from Pittsburgh had spent its time parading and building a few posts to facilitate its future designs. This information, which came from the Falls of the Ohio, disappointed us greatly.

One Denny, an inhabitant of Cahokia, was seized by Major Bowman for sending by the Indians to his friend in Detroit a letter containing dangerous information. His message was intercepted, and he was tied to the tail of a cart and driven through the town, receiving a lash at every door. He was also branded in the hand for other misdemeanors. This was the first and the severest punishment inflicted by us on any of the inhabitants. It was necessary at this time to convince the people that we were capable of extremes either way, and that the good treatment we had heretofore shown them was due to the principles of the government.

For some time past we had received no information from Vincennes. Since the post went fortnightly we began to feel that something was wrong. We sent out some scouts, but they did not return, and we continued in a state of suspense. I had prepared to set out from Kaskaskia to Cahokia, but for several days the weather was bad. At length I set out in a snow storm which gave promise of clearing up, and which did so in about half an hour. We noticed that six or seven men had passed some distance along the road since the snow had ceased. We supposed it to be some of the townsmen, but we wondered what they could be about. I had several gentlemen accompanying me in chairs. Approaching the hill near the river, one of these sank in a swamp, and the gentleman who rode in it was some time in getting out, as the others would not permit any assistance to be given until after their laughter had subsided. We went cheerfully on to Prairie du Rocher, twelve miles from Kaskaskia, where I intended to spend the evening at Captain Barbour's. After supper a dance was proposed. While it was at its height an express came to me that late that evening a party of white men and Indians had come to some negroes, who were up the Kaskaskia River cutting wood, and after asking a number of questions told the negroes that they had a party of eight hundred men a few miles away, and intended to attack the fort that night. They threatened the negroes with death if they should reveal this information and went away. The negroes told it and the express was dispatched for me. This report sounded to us like the truth. For some time past our suspicions had been aroused; we recalled the various reports of the Indians, the failure of our scouts to return, and the tracks we had seen in the road. The inhabitants of Prairie du Rocher were greatly alarmed. They urged me to cross the Mississippi to the Spanish side for protection, saying the fort must already be invested.

I laughed at the idea, and much to their amusement resolved to attempt to enter the fort. I ordered our horses, and borrowing clothes to dress my men in the garb of hunters set out, making a pretense of being greatly amused over the situation. The ground was covered with snow and the moon shone brightly. I took the express along with me in order to have some time for thought, and in about a quarter of an hour wrote a card to Major Bowman at Cahokia, directing him to come with his company and all the volunteers he could raise. I told him to be cautious, and if he should find he could not render any service to us he should retreat to Ste. Genevieve and act as circumstances might dictate. The express was an expert woodsman, and was mounted on the best horse we had. He was ordered to run the horse as long as it could go faster than he could walk; then to abandon the animal and make the best of his way on foot.

We continued on our way, making a detour from the road whenever we came to any woods which might serve as a covert for an enemy. Our design in dressing as woodsmen in leggings and capotes, with handkerchiefs tied on our heads, was to leave our horses in case we should find the enemy had actually invested the fort, enter their lines and fight with the Indians (who we thought would not be likely to distinguish us from the English) until we could make good our way to a certain ravine near one of the angles of the fort where there was a small sally port. Here we could easily make ourselves known, and probably draw some of them into it. Such was our plan in this seemingly desperate situation. As we drew near the town all was silent. We approached cautiously, and making a circuit, perceived from the condition of the snow that no body of men had entered the town. Accordingly we went in, to the great joy of every one. I found that every preparation had been made and every circumstance, particularly the character of the conversation with the negroes, caused us to believe that the enemy was in the neighborhood. The night passed, however, without any further alarm, and it was generally supposed that the snow had prevented the attack.

I spent the night in various reflections. I knew that it was impossible for us to defend the town, or to hold out in the fort, but I was in hopes of baffling their enterprise and frightening them away by circulating a plausible report (since they must have taken Vincennes before they could get to us) that we had received full information of their proceedings, and had sent an express to Kentucky for an army to advance and cut off their retreat. Since according to the report of the negroes most of the inhabitants of the town were severely threatened, I was afraid they would propose defending it; but that nothing should appear wanting on our part, I sent for the principal men and put the question to them, desiring them to speak their sentiments freely. After some deliberation they told me that they thought it prudent to remain neutral. This was certainly a judicious resolution, and was what I desired, but I proceeded to make capital of it. I pretended to be in a passion, and ordered them to their homes, saying I had no further business with them, and that I expected they would soon see their town in flames. They went away and some of the young men voluntarily joined us. Some of them privately advised that all the wood in town should be ordered into the garrison, but I gave them a short answer, and told them we had plenty of provisions. Several houses being close to the walls of the fort, the inhabitants were told to vacate them as they would be burned at once. A large barn full of grain that stood a short distance away was immediately set on fire without anything being taken out of it, and soon other small buildings were torn down and carried into the fort for fuel, while preparations were made to fire still other buildings.

All was now confusion, the town on fire, the women and children screaming, and the inhabitants moving out. I keenly felt their distress. Some of them begged to know how much of the town I intended to burn, so that they might move their goods out of danger. They were told that it was far from our wish to destroy more than was absolutely necessary. They must realize that at a time like this it was our duty to do whatever might be necessary to promote our safety. I said that although I knew the enemy would soon be intercepted by an army from Kentucky, they might, meanwhile, do us much damage if we did not take necessary precautions. We meant to destroy the provisions only to prevent them from falling into the hands of the enemy. This they must confess was justifiable, but as the wind was unfavorable no more buildings would be set on fire till it shifted. They went away, and we waited to see what the result of our procedure would be. In a very short time we observed the carts begin to move, and within two or three hours we had upwards of two months' provisions in store.

Our policy was, aside from getting the provisions, to make ourselves appear as daring as possible. We therefore desired the people to stop, telling them that perhaps the report was false, and that the scouts would soon return, when we would know better how to proceed. They did so in a short time, and informed me that they discovered the trail of seventy or eighty men who were apparently directing their course towards Vincennes, but that there was no sign of a formidable force in the neighborhood. Things now began to quiet down. The next day Major Bowman arrived with a considerable force of men and we began to pluck up our courage.

It was now conjectured that Vincennes was in the hands of the enemy and that the party which had been seen in our neighborhood had been sent from that place on some errand or other; the snowfall had rendered it impossible for them to remain undiscovered, since they were compelled to hunt to obtain food, and they had given the alarm in order that they might gain time to escape. We afterward learned that this was substantially the case. It was a party composed chiefly of Indians which Governor Hamilton, who was now in possession of Vincennes, had sent out with careful instructions to lie in the neighborhood of the Illinois towns until they could find an opportunity to make me prisoner. Under no circumstances were they to kill me, but in case of success were to treat me with every courtesy. They were to furnish me with a horse for the return journey and were to permit me to take such amusement as I should desire en route, but I was always to be attended by persons mounted on better horses than my own. Thus I was to be a prisoner of state in the hands of the savages.

By some means or other (I never could be entirely satisfied from whom) this party learned of my intention to pay a visit to the garrison at Cahokia. Accordingly they concealed themselves behind a hill near the road about three miles above Kaskaskia, keeping a small lookout in advance. The day I set out these fellows had advanced closer to the town than usual. The snow coming on, they had returned to their camp, walking some distance in the road, which occasioned the tracks we saw. The country being very open in this vicinity and we riding very fast, made it impossible for them to return so as to alarm the camp without being discovered, and they therefore secreted themselves behind some logs and bushes within seventy or eighty yards of the ravine where we were delayed by the swamping of the chair. They reported that they could have surprised and taken most of us, but not being able to distinguish me from the rest, as we were all muffled up, they were afraid to fire for fear of killing me. I suppose the truth was that they were afraid to reveal themselves as we were nearly twice their number, and even our servants were fully armed. The bad weather proved to be our salvation as they did not expect us to come out and the greater part of them had returned to camp, leaving only seven men on outpost duty.

Perceiving that their hopes were now blasted, and that they could not remain longer without being discovered, they fell in with the negroes with the design of creating such an alarm as should give them time to get away, and in this they were entirely successful. The instructions given by Governor Hamilton to this party was one of the principal causes of the respect shown him by our officers when he fell into our hands; but his treatment in Virginia was quite different and highly unsatisfactory to them, as they thought it in some measure involved their honor.

To return to our subject, it was concluded to send additional scouts to Vincennes, and in the meantime to prepare ourselves for action. Being fully confident that a change either in our favor or against us would shortly take place, we desired to strengthen ourselves as much as possible. The volunteers who had accompanied Major Bowman from Cahokia were presented with an elegant stand of colors and sent home. Those of them who were but poorly armed were outfitted from our stores, while presents were made to the others by way of acknowledgment of the good will they had shown on the present occasion. They paraded about town with their new flag and equipment and looked upon themselves as superior to the young fellows of Kaskaskia; it caused so much animosity between the two parties that it did not subside until I intervened, somewhat later, when it suited my purpose to do so, and by a little strategy reunited them.

After making every arrangement that we thought most conducive to our safety Major Bowman returned to Cahokia and we awaited in suspense the return of our scouts. I thought that if we should find there was no probability of retaining our posts I would abandon them upon the approach of the enemy and return to Kentucky where I would raise a force (the population having considerably increased) sufficient to cut off the retreat of the English to Detroit, since I knew the Indians, who were not fond of long campaigns, would abandon them. However, on the 29th of January, 1779, Mr. Vigo,[39] a Spanish merchant, arrived from Vincennes, bringing the information that Governor Hamilton with thirty regulars and fifty French volunteers, besides Indian agents, interpreters, and boatmen to a considerable num-

[39] François Vigo was a Sardinian who, after resigning from the Spanish army entered the fur trade, with headquarters at St. Louis. He was a business partner of the Spanish governor of Upper Louisiana. He threw his influence upon the American side, and both on his own behalf and through his influence with Governor DeLeyba gave powerful aid to Clark. In so doing he incurred heavy expenditures which he never recovered, although he lived until 1836. Not until 1875 did the United States government reimburse his heirs for the money advanced in its behalf almost a century before.

ber, and about four hundred Indians had taken that post in December. The season being so far advanced, he had thought it impossible to reach the Illinois and had sent some of his Indians to Kentucky to keep watch of the Ohio River and disbanded the rest. All were to meet again in the spring, drive us out of the Illinois country, and in conjunction with their southern friends attack Kentucky in a body. All the goods belonging to the merchants at Vincennes were taken for the king's use. They were repairing the fort and expecting a reinforcement to arrive from Detroit in the spring. Mr. Vigo stated that they appeared to have plenty of stores of all kinds, and that they were strict in their discipline, but he did not believe they were under much apprehension of a visit from us and he thought that if we could get there undiscovered we might capture the place. In short, we received all the information from this gentleman that we could desire as he had enjoyed a good opportunity to inform himself and had taken pains to do so with a view to bringing the report to us.

We now saw that we were in a very critical situation, cut off as we were from all intercourse with the home government. We perceived that Governor Hamilton, by the junction of his northern and southern Indians, would be at the head of such a force in the spring that nothing in this quarter could withstand him. Kentucky must fall immediately and it would be fortunate if the disaster ended here. Even if we should immediately make good our retreat to Kentucky we were convinced that it would be too late even to raise a force sufficient to save that colony, as all the men in it, united to the troops we had, would not suffice, and to get succor in time from the Virginia and Pennsylvania frontiers was out of the question. We saw but one alternative which was to attack the enemy in his stronghold. If we were successful we would thereby save the whole American cause. If unsuccessful, the consequence would be nothing worse than if we should not make the attempt. We were encouraged by the thought of the magnitude of the consequences that would attend our success. The season of the year was also favorable to our design, since the enemy could not suppose that we would be so mad as to attempt a march of eighty leagues through a drowned country in the depth of winter. They would, therefore, be off their guard and would not think it worth while, probably, to keep scouts out. If we could make good our advance to Vincennes we might probably surprise and overcome them, while if we should fail, the country would be in no worse situation than if we had not made the attempt. This and many other similar reasons induced us to resolve to attempt the enterprise, which met with the approbation of every man among us.

Orders were immediately issued for making the necessary preparations. The whole country took fire and every order, such as preparing provisions, encouraging volunteers, etc., was executed with cheerfulness by the inhabitants. Since we had an abundance of supplies, every man was equipped with whatever he could desire to withstand the coldest weather. Knowing that the Wabash would probably overflow its banks to a width of five or six miles and that it would be dangerous to build vessels in the neighborhood of the enemy, I concluded, both to obviate this and to convey our artillery and stores, to send around by water a vessel strong enough to force her way, as she could be attacked only by water (unless she should choose otherwise) since the whole of the lowlands was under water and she might keep away from any heights along the river. A large Mississippi boat was immediately purchased and completely fitted out as a galley, mounting two four-pounders and four large swivels, and manned by forty-six men under the command of John Rogers.[40] He set sail on February 4th, with orders to force his way up the Wabash as high as the mouth of White River, and there

[40] John Rogers was a cousin of Clark. He saw service in the earlier years of the Revolution, and in 1778 became second-lieutenant in Captain Helm's company on Clark's Kaskaskia expedition. As noted here, Clark placed him in command of the war galley sent against Vincennes. After its capture Rogers was sent to convey the British prisoners to Williams-

secrete himself until further orders; if he should find himself discovered he was to do the enemy all the damage he could without running too great risk of losing his vessel. He was not to leave the river until he had abandoned hope of our arrival by land, but he was strictly enjoined to so conduct himself as to give rise to no suspicion of our expected approach.

We placed great dependence in this vessel. She was far superior to anything the enemy could fit out unless they should build a new one, and at the worst if we were discovered we could build a number of large perogues, such as they possessed, to attend her. With such a fleet we could annoy the enemy very much and if we saw it to be to our interest could force a landing. At any rate it would be some time before they could match us on the water. Having been in a state of suspense for some time past we had made preparations in part for some such event as this and these were now soon completed. The inhabitants of Kaskaskia had been somewhat cowed since the affair of the supposedly impending siege and nothing was said to them on the subject

burg. In Virginia he was accorded public honors for his services and was made captain of a mounted troop for the western service. Returning to the west he served in Montgomery's Rock River expedition, and in the autumn was appointed commandant of Kaskaskia. He returned to Virginia the following summer, and died at Richmond in 1794.

of volunteering until the arrival of the volunteers from Cahokia. We gave these an expensive entertainment to which they invited all their Kaskaskia acquaintances. During its progress all minor differences were composed and by twelve o'clock the next day application had been made for permission to raise a company at Kaskaskia. This was granted and before nightfall the company was enrolled, all of the townsmen having exerted themselves in order to wipe out the memory of their former coolness.

Everything being ready on the 5th of February, after receiving a lecture and absolution from a priest, we crossed the Kaskaskia River with 170 men and at a distance of about three miles encamped until February 8. When we again resumed the advance the weather was wet and a part of the country was covered with several inches of water. Progress under these conditions was difficult and fatiguing although, fortunately, it was not very cold considering the time of year. My object now was to keep the men in good spirits. I permitted them to shoot game on all occasions and to feast on it like Indians at a war dance, each company taking turns in inviting the other to its feast. A feast was held every night, the company that was to give it being always supplied with horses for laying in a sufficient store of meat in the course of the day. I myself and my principal officers conducted ourselves like woodsmen, shouting now and then and running through the mud and water the same as the men themselves.

Thus, insensible of their hardships and without complaining, our men were conducted through difficulties far surpassing anything we had ever experienced before this to the banks of the Little Wabash, which we reached on February 13. There are here two streams three miles apart, and the distance from the bank of one to the opposite bank of the other is five miles. This whole distance we found covered with some three feet of water, being never less than two, and frequently four feet in depth. I went into camp on an elevation at the bank of the river and gave the troops permission to amuse themselves. For some time I viewed with consternation this expanse of water; then accusing myself of irresolution, without holding any consultation over the situation or permitting anyone else to do so in my presence, I immediately set to work. I ordered a perogue to be constructed at once and acted as though crossing the water would be only a bit of diversion. Since but few of the men could find employment at a time, pains were taken to devise amusement for the rest in order to keep up their spirits. However, the men were well prepared for the undertaking before us as they had frequently waded farther than we must now, although seldom in water more than half-leg deep.

My eagerness to cross steadily increased, since I perceived that to do so would precipitate us into a forlorn hope; if after this was accomplished the men should begin to think seriously of what they had undergone they would abandon all thought of retreat, preferring to undergo any difficulty which offered a prospect of success, rather than to attempt a retreat involving the certainty of encountering all they had already endured, while in the event of freezing weather retreat would be altogether impracticable until the ice should become firm enough to support them. On the evening of the 14th our boat was completed and I sent a crew of men to explore the drowned lands and find if possible some spot of dry land on the bank of the second little river. They found a place about half an acre in extent and marked the trees from it back to the camp. They returned with a very favorable report, having received private instructions from me in advance as to what they should say.

Fortunately for us the 15th chanced to be a warm, moist day considering the season. The channel of the river where we were encamped was about thirty yards wide and the opposite bank was under three feet of water. Here we built a scaffold and the baggage was put upon it and ferried across, while our horses swam the channel and at the scaffold were again loaded with the baggage. By this time the soldiers had also been brought across and we took up our march, our boat being loaded with men who were sick. We moved on cheerfully, expecting every moment to see dry land, but none was discovered until we came to the small spots already mentioned. The river channel here being smaller than the first one, the troops immediately crossed it and marched on in the water as before in order to gain the nearest height they could discover. Our horses and baggage crossed the second river in the same manner as the first and followed in the trail of the troops (since their tracks could not be seen in the water they marked the trees as they proceeded). Evening found us encamped on a handsome elevation, the men in high spirits, each one laughing at some one else over some mishap that had occurred in the course of this ferrying business, as they called it, and all together over the great exploit they had performed. A comical little drummer had afforded them great diversion by floating on his drum and other tricks. Such incidents greatly encouraged them and they really began to regard themselves as superior to other men and as persons whom neither floods nor seasons could stop. All their conversation was now about what they would do when they could charge the enemy and they began to talk about the main Wabash as a creek, not doubting but such men as they were would find a way to cross it. Their spirits rose to such a pitch that they soon took Vincennes and divided the spoil, and before bed time were far advanced on the road to Detroit.

This optimism was of course gratifying to those of us who were indulging in more serious reflections. We were now in the enemy's country, as it were, with no possibility of retreating in case the enemy should discover and overpower us (except by means of our galley if we should fall in with her). We were now convinced that all of the low country along the Wabash was flooded, and that the enemy could easily come to us if they should discover us and care to risk an action. Should they not do this we entertained no doubt of crossing the river by some means or other. In case Captain Rogers had not reached his station according to his appointment we would endeavor to steal some boats from the houses opposite the town, and we flattered ourselves that all would be well and we would march on in high spirits.

On the seventeenth I despatched Mr. Kennedy with three men to cross the River Embarrass, which is six miles from Vincennes, charging him to procure, if possible, some boats in the neighborhood of the town, but chiefly to obtain some information if he could do so in safety. He went and on reaching the river found that the country between it and the Wabash was flooded. We proceeded down below the mouth of the Embarrass, vainly attempting to reach the banks of the Wabash. Finding a dry spot we encamped late at night and in the morning were gratified at hearing for the first time the morning gun of the British garrison. We resumed our march and about two o'clock in the afternoon of the eighteenth gained the banks of the Wabash three leagues below the town and went into camp.

I now sent four men across the river on a raft to find land if possible, proceed to the town, and purloin some canoes. Captain McCarty set out with a few men the next morning with a little canoe he had made for the same purpose. Both parties returned unsuccessful; the first was unable to make land, and the Captain was driven back by the appearance of a camp. I immediately despatched the canoe down the river to meet the galley, carrying orders for it to proceed day and night. Meanwhile, determined to have as many strings to my bow as possible I directed the men to build canoes in a sheltered place. I had not yet given up hope of our boat arriving; in case she should, these canoes would augment our fleet; should she not come before they were ready, they would answer our purpose without her.

Many of our volunteers began for the first time to despair and some to talk of returning but our situation was now such that I was past all uneasiness. I merely laughed at them; without persuading or ordering them to desist from such an attempt I told them I would be glad if they would go out and kill some deer. They departed puzzled over my conduct. My own men knew that I had no idea of abandoning an enterprise for want of provisions so long as there were plenty of good horses in our possession and I knew that our volunteers could be detained without the use of force for a few days, by which time our fate would be determined. I conducted myself in such a manner as to lead everyone to believe I had no doubt of success. This kept up their spirits, and the hunters being out, they had hope of momentarily obtaining a supply of food, besides the expectation of the arrival of the galley. I perceived that if we should not be discovered for two days we would effect the passage of the river.

On the twentieth the water guard decoyed a boat ashore having five Frenchmen and some provisions on board. These men were on their way down river to join a party of hunters. They informed us that we had been discovered and that the inhabitants were well disposed towards us. They said the fort had been completed and greatly strengthened, and that the number of men in it was about the same as when Mr. Vigo left Vincennes. In short, they gave us all the information we desired, even telling us of two boats that were adrift up the river, one of which Captain Worthington recovered.

Having now two small boats, early on the morning of the twenty-first, abandoning our baggage, we began crossing over the troops and landing them on a small elevation called the Mamel. While engaged in searching foı a passage Captain J. Williams gave chase to a canoe but could not take it. The men we had captured said it was impossible for us to make the town that night or at all with our boats. Recalling what we had done, however, we thought otherwise, and pushing into the water marched a league, frequently in water to our arm pits, to what is called the upper Mamel. Here we encamped our men, still in good spirits from the hope of soon putting an end to their fatigue and realizing their desire to come into contact with the enemy.

This last march through the water was so far superior to anything our prisoners had conceived of that they were backward about saying anything further. They told us the nearest land was the Sugar Camp, a small league away on the bank of the river. A canoe was sent off to it and returned with the report that we could not pass. I now went myself and sounding the water found it as deep as my neck. I returned with the thought of having the men transported to the Sugar Camp in the canoes, which I knew would consume the entire day and the ensuing night since the boats would pass but slowly through the bushes. To men half starved the loss of so much time was a serious matter and I would now have given a good deal for a day's provisions or for one of our horses.

I returned but slowly to the troops in order to gain time for reflection. On our arrival all ran to hear our report and every eye was fixed on me. Unfortunately I spoke in a serious manner to one of the officers and without knowing what I had said all were thrown into a state of alarm, running from one to another and bewailing their situation. For about a minute I stood looking upon their confusion and then, whispering to those close by to do as I did I quickly scooped up some water with my hand, poured some powder into it, and blacking my face, raised the war whoop. I marched into the water. The party gazed at me for an instant and then like a flock of sheep fell in, one behind the other, without saying a word. I ordered the men who were near me to strike up one of their favorite songs. It soon passed down the line and all went on cheerfully. I now intended to have them ferried across the deepest part of the water but when we continued out about waist deep one of the men told me he thought he felt a path. We found it to be so and concluded that it kept to the highest ground. This proved to be the case, and by taking pains to follow it we reached the Sugar Camp without the least difficulty. Here we found about half an acre of dry ground, or at any rate ground not under water, and on it we took up our lodging.

The Frenchmen whom we had captured on the river appeared to be uneasy about our situation. They begged that they might be permitted to go to town by night in two canoes, saying they would bring us provisions from their own homes without the possibility of any one finding it out. They asked that some of our men should go with them as a pledge of their good conduct. It was impossible, they said, for us to march from this place until the water should fall. This would require several days, since the plain in front of us for a distance of three miles was covered too deep to march over. Some of our men urged that this be done, but I refused to permit it. I have never been able to account satisfactorily either to myself or anyone else for thus refusing a proposition which was apparently so easy to execute and of such great advantage to us, but something seemed to tell me it should not be done and it was not.

During most of this march the weather was warm and moist for the season. This was the coldest night we had and in the morning the ice was one-half or three-fourths of an inch deep in still water and close to shore. The morning was the finest we had had on our entire march. Shortly after sunrise I addressed the men. What I said to them I do not now remember, but it may be easily imagined by anyone who can understand my affection for them at that time. I concluded by informing them that by surmounting the plain, now in full view, and reaching the woods opposite they would put an end to their suffering and in a few hours would have sight of their long-wished-for goal. Without waiting for any reply I stepped into the water and a hurrah was raised. We commonly marched through the water in single file as it was much easier to advance in this way. When about a third of the men had entered I halted them and further to prove the men, and because I had some suspicion of three or four of them, I called to Major Bowman to fall into the rear with twenty-five men and to put to death any of the men who refused to march, saying that we wished to have no such person among us. The whole force raised a cry of approbation and on we went. This was the most trying difficulty of all we had experienced. I had fifteen or twenty of the strongest men follow after me and, judging from my own sensations what must be those of the men, on reaching the middle of the plain where the water was about knee deep I realized that I was failing. There being no trees or bushes here for the men to support themselves by, I did not doubt but that many of the weaker ones would be drowned. I therefore ordered the canoes to make the land, discharge their loads, and then ply backwards and forwards with all possible diligence, picking up the men. To encourage the party I sent some of the strongest men ahead with orders to pass the word back when they reached a certain distance that the water was getting shallower, and on approaching the woods to cry out "Land." This stratagem produced the desired effect. Encouraged by it the men exerted themselves to the limit of their ability, the weaker holding on to the stronger ones and frequently one man being upheld by two. This was a great advantage to the weak, but the water, instead of getting shallower, became continually deeper. On reaching the woods, where they expected land, the water was up to my shoulders. Nevertheless, gaining these woods was a matter of great importance. All the weak and short men clung to the trees and floated on logs until they were taken off by the canoes. The strong and tall men got ashore and started fires. Many would reach the bank and fall with their bodies half in the water, not being able to support themselves outside it. This was a delightful spot of dry ground about ten acres in extent. We soon found, however, that the fires did us no good and that the only way to restore the men was for two strong ones to take a weak one by the arms and exercise him. The day was delightful and by this means they soon recovered.

A piece of fortune now befell us which seemed to be designed by Providence. Some Indian Squaws and children, coming up to the town in a canoe, took a short cut through this part of the plain and were discovered by our canoes while they were out after the men. Our boats gave chase to the canoe and captured it, finding on board nearly half a quarter of buffalo besides some corn, tallow, and kettles. This was an invaluable prize to us. We immediately made some broth and served it to the weaker men. By the exercise of great care most of the men obtained a little, but many of them would not taste it, giving it instead to the weaker ones and saying something encouraging to their comrades. By afternoon this little refreshment, with the addition of fine weather, gave new life to the troops. Crossing a deep narrow lake in the canoes and marching some distance we came to a copse of timber called Warriors Island. We were now in full view of the fort and town which were distant about two miles and with not a shrub between us and the place. Every one feasted his eyes and forgot that he had suffered anything. All that had passed was attributed to good policy and was nothing that a man could not bear and a soldier had no right to think, etc. Thus they passed from one extreme to another, as commonly under such circumstances.

Now came the real test of our ability. The plain between us and the town was not a perfect level, and the sunken ground was covered with water full of ducks. We observed several men out on horseback shooting ducks about half a mile away and sent off several of our active young men to decoy and capture one of them in such a manner as not to alarm the rest. The information we obtained from this person was similar to that received from those we had taken on the river, with the exception of the news that the British had that evening completed the wall of the fort and that there were a large number of Indians in the town. Our situation was now sufficiently critical. We were within full view of a town which contained upwards of six hundred men, counting soldiers, inhabitants, and Indians, with no possibility of retreat open to us in case of defeat. The crew of the galley, although numbering less than fifty men, would have constituted a reinforcement of great importance to our little army. But we would not permit ourselves to dwell on this. We were now in the situation I had been laboring to attain. The idea of being taken prisoner was foreign to almost all of our men. In the event of capture they looked forward to being tortured by the savages. Our fate was now to be determined, probably within the next few hours, and we knew that nothing but the boldest conduct would insure success. I knew that some of the inhabitants wished us well, while many more were lukewarm to the interest of the British and Americans alike. I also learned that the Grand Chief, the son of Tobacco, had within a few days openly declared in council with the British that he was a brother and friend of the Big Knives. These circumstances were in our favor. Many hunters were going back and forth and there was little probability of our remaining undiscovered until dark. Accordingly I determined to bring matters to an issue at once, and writing the following address to the inhabitants sent it off by the prisoner we had just taken:

TO THE INHABITANTS OF VINCENNES—

Gentlemen: Being now within two miles of your village with my army determined to take your fort this night, and not being willing to surprise you, I am taking the measure of requesting such of you as are true citizens and desirous of enjoying the liberty I bring you to remain quietly in your houses. If there are any that are friends of the King of England I desire them instantly to repair to the fort and there join his troops and fight like men; and if any that do not repair to the garrison shall hereafter be discovered they may depend upon being severely punished. Those, on the other hand, who are true friends to Liberty may expect to be well treated. I once more request that they keep out of the streets, for every person found under arms upon my arrival will be treated as an enemy.

I entertained conflicting ideas as to what would be the result of this letter. I knew, however, that it could do us no damage, but that it would encourage our friends, cause those who were lukewarm to take a decided stand, and astonish our enemies. I felt sure that they would suppose our information to be valid and our forces so numerous that we were certain of success; that they would suppose our army to be from Kentucky, and not from the Illinois, as it would be deemed impossible for troops to march from the latter place; and would think that my name had been employed by way of subterfuge (this they firmly believed until the next morning, when I was pointed out to them by a person in the fort who knew me well) or that we were a reconnoitering party who only employed this stratagem in order to gain time to effect our retreat. This latter idea I knew would soon be done away. Several gentlemen sent their compliments to their friends under borrowed names which were well known at Vincennes and who were supposed to have been in Kentucky. The soldiers were all given instructions that when speaking of our numbers their common conversation should be of such character as to induce a stranger overhearing it to suppose we had nearly a thousand men. We anxiously watched the messenger until he reached the town and in a few minutes we could perceive with the aid of our glasses a stirring about in every street and large numbers running or riding out into the commons, intent as we supposed upon viewing us. This proved to be the case, but to our great surprise nothing occurred to indicate that the garrison had been alarmed. Neither drum nor guns were heard. This led us to suppose that the information obtained from our prisoner was false and that the enemy was already aware of our presence and prepared to meet us. Every man among us had been impatient for the moment which was now at hand. Shortly before sunset we advanced, displaying ourselves in full view of the crowds in the town. We were plunging headlong either to certain destruction or to success. No middle ground was even thought of. I said but little to the men, aside from emphasizing the necessity for obedience. I knew they did not need encouraging and that anything might be attempted with them that it was possible for such a number of men, perfectly cool, properly disciplined, pleased with the prospect before them, and greatly attached to their officers, to perform. All declared themselves convinced that implicit obedience to orders would alone insure success, and that they hoped anyone who should violate them would immediately be put to death. To a person in my situation such language as this from the soldiers was exceedingly agreeable.

We advanced slowly in full view of the town, but as it was a matter of some consequence to make ourselves appear as formidable as possible, on leaving our place of concealment we marched and countermarched in a fashion calculated to magnify our numbers. Every person who had undertaken to enroll volunteers in the Illinois had been presented with a stand of colors and these, ten or twelve in number, they had brought along with them. We now displayed these to the best possible advantage, and since the plain through which we were marching was not perfectly level but was dotted with elevations rising seven or eight feet above the common level and running in an oblique direction to our line of march towards the town, we took advantage of one of these to march our men along the low ground so that only the colors (which had been fixed to long poles procured for the purpose) could be seen above the height. While we lay on Warriors' Island our young Frenchmen had decoyed and captured several hunters with their horses; I therefore caused our officers, mounted on these, to ride in and out in order more completely to deceive the enemy. In this manner we advanced, directing our march in such fashion that darkness fell before we had proceeded more than half way to the town. We then suddenly altered our direction and crossed some ponds where they could not suspect our presence. About eight o'clock we gained the heights in the rear of the town. There being still no enemy in sight, I became impatient to solve the mystery. I ordered Lieutenant Bailey with fourteen men to advance and open fire on the fort while the main body moved in a different direction and took possession of the strongest part of the town. The firing now commenced against the fort, but since drunken Indians often saluted it after nightfall, the garrison did not suppose it to be from an enemy until one of the men, lighting his match, was shot down through a porthole. The drums now sounded and the conflict was fairly joined on both sides. I sent reinforcements to assist in the attack on the garrison, while other dispositions were being made in the town.

We now found that the garrison had known nothing of our approach. Having finished the fort that evening, they had indulged in games for a time and then retired just before the arrival of my letter. As it was almost time for roll call when its terms were made known many of the inhabitants were afraid to show themselves outside their houses and not one had dared to inform the garrison. Our friends, meanwhile, had rushed to the commons and other convenient places from which to view the pleasing sight afforded by our approach. The garrison had noticed this action and inquired the reason for it, but a satisfactory excuse had been offered and since a portion of the town lay between our line of march and the fort we had not been seen by the sentinels on the walls. Some time before this Captain W. Shannon[41] and another man had been captured by one of their scouting parties and brought to the fort that same evening. This party had discovered some signs of us at the Sugar Camp and, supposing it to be a party of observation

[41] Captain William Shannon was commissary and quartermaster of the Illinois battalion.

which intended to land on the height some distance below the town, Captain La Mothe[42] had been sent to intercept them. When the people were asked the reason of their unusual excitement they had said they were looking at him.

Several persons whose loyalty was under suspicion had been imprisoned in the fort, among them Mr. Moses Henry.[43] Under the pretense of carrying some provisions to him Mrs. Henry went and whispered to him the news of our arrival and what she had seen. This Mr. Henry conveyed to his fellow prisoners. It gave them much pleasure, particularly Captain Helm, who amused himself greatly during the siege and I believe did much damage. We had a scanty supply of ammu-

[42] Guillaume La Mothe was a native of Canada who subsequent to the French and Indian War became a trader in the neighborhood of Detroit. In 1777 he became captain of a scouting party, and the following year accompanied Hamilton to Vincennes. With his chief he was sent prisoner by Clark to Virginia, where he was kept in close confinement until exchanged in 1781. He returned to the Northwest and from 1792 to 1796 served as interpreter at Mackinac. When the Americans took over the place in 1796, La Mothe retired with the British to St. Joseph, where he died in 1799.

[43] Henry was a resident of Vincennes. Clark made him Indian agent and Henry shortly accompanied an expedition up the Wabash to capture a British convoy. In 1781 Henry was still living in Vincennes, where he died at some time prior to 1790, leaving a widow and children.

nition since most of our stores had been put on board the galley. Though her crew were small such a reinforcement would have been invaluable to us at this juncture. Fortunately, however, at the time it had been announced that all of the goods in the town were to be seized for the King's use (the owners were to receive bills of credit in return), Colonel Le Gras, Major Bosseron, and others had buried the greater part of their powder and ball. This ammunition was immediately produced and we found ourselves well supplied by these gentlemen. The Tobacco's son, being in town with a number of his warriors, immediately mustered them and indicated a desire to join us, saying that by morning he would have a hundred men. I thanked him for his friendly disposition but told him we were already strong enough and desired him to refrain. I said we would discuss the matter in the morning, but since we knew there were a number of Indians hostile to us in and about the town some confusion might result if our men should mix in the dark. I expressed the hope that we might be favored with his counsel and company during the night and this proved agreeable to him.

The garrison was now completely surrounded and the firing continued without intermission (except for about fifteen minutes shortly before dawn) until nine o'clock the following morning. Our entire force, with the exception of fifty men kept as a reserve in case of some emergency, participated in the attack, being joined by a few young men. I had acquainted myself fully with the situation of the fort and town and had detailed information concerning each of them. The cannon were on the upper floors of strong blockhouses located at each angle of the fort eleven feet above the ground, and the portholes were so badly cut that our troops lay under their fire within twenty or thirty yards of the walls. The enemy did no damage except to the buildings of the town, some of which were badly shattered, while their musket fire in the dark was employed in vain against woodsmen who were sheltered behind the palings of the houses (the gardens of Vincennes were close to the fort and for about two-thirds of the way around them were fenced with good pickets firmly set in the ground and about six feet high. Where these were lacking breastworks for the troops were soon made by tearing down old houses and garden fences, so that the troops within the fort enjoyed but little advantage over those outside; and not knowing the number of the enemy, they thought themselves in a worse situation than they actually were), river banks, and ditches, and did us no damage except for the wounding of a man or two.

Since we could not afford to lose any of our men, great pains were taken to keep them sufficiently sheltered and to maintain a hot fire against the fort in order to intimidate the enemy as well as to destroy them. The embrasures for their cannon were frequently closed, for our riflemen finding the true direction would pour in such volleys when they were open that the artillerymen could not stand to the guns. Seven or eight of them were shot down in a short time. Our men frequently taunted the enemy in order to provoke them into opening the portholes and firing the cannon so that they might have the pleasure of cutting them down with their rifles. Fifty rifles would be leveled the instant the port flew open, and had the garrison stood to their artillery most of them, I believe, would have been destroyed during the night as the greater part of our men, lying within thirty yards of the walls, and behind some houses, were as well sheltered as those within the fort and were much more expert in this mode of fighting. The enemy fired at the flash of our guns, but our men would change their positions the moment they had fired. On the instant of the least appearance at one of their loopholes a dozen guns would be fired at it. At times an irregular fire as hot as could be maintained was poured in from different directions for several minutes. This would be continually succeeded by a scattering fire at the portholes and a great uproar and laughter would be raised by the reserve parties in different parts of the town to give the impression that they had only fired on the fort for a few minutes for amusement, while those who were keeping up a continuous fire were being regularly relieved.

Conduct such as this kept the garrison in a constant state of alarm. They did not know what moment they might be stormed or sapped as they could plainly see that we had thrown up entrenchments across the streets and we frequently appeared to be busily engaged on the bank of the river, which was within thirty feet of the wall. We knew the location of the magazine and Captain Bowman began some work designed to blow it up when our artillery should arrive. Knowing that we were daily liable to be overpowered by the numerous bands of Indians on the river in case they should again heartily join the enemy (as to the likelihood of which we were yet uninformed) we resolved to lose no time, but to gain possession of the fort as soon possible. Unless the vessel should arrive sooner, we determined to undermine the fort the following night and fixed upon the spot and the plan of executing this work, which we intended to begin the next day.

The Indians belonging to the different hostile tribes had left the town and neighborhood but Captain La Mothe still hovered about, waiting an opportunity to make good his way into the fort. Parties of our men attempted in vain to surprise him, although a few of his men were captured, among them one Maisonville, a famous Indian partisan. Two lads who had captured him led him to a position in the street and fought from behind him as a breastwork, supposing the enemy would not fire at them for fear of killing him. An officer who discovered them at this amusement ordered them to untie him and take him away under guard. This they did, but were so inhuman as to remove part of his scalp on the way, but did him no other harm.[44] Since almost all of those who were most active in the department of Detroit were either inside the fort or with Captain La Mothe I became uneasy for fear he would not fall into our hands since I knew he would retire if he could not effect his purpose in the course of the night. Perceiving that unless some unforeseen accident should occur the fort must inevitably be ours, and that a reinforcement of twenty men, although considerable to them, could not be of any great moment to us in the present posture of our affairs, and knowing that we had weakened them by killing or wounding many of their gunners, I concluded after some deliberation

[44] Governor Hamilton, in his official report, states that Maisonville was betrayed into Clark's hands by his cousin; and that the scalping was committed by a soldier acting under Clark's orders to scalp him and that these were relaxed upon the appeal of a brother of Maisonville — who had attached himself to the Americans. Maisonville was sent with Hamilton to prison in Virginia. The hardships and ill treatment he endured there so wrought upon his mind that he finally sought escape from them by committing suicide.

to risk the reinforcement in preference to his going again among the Indians. I knew the garrison had at least a month's supply of provisons and if it could hold out he might in the course of this time do us great damage.

Shortly before dawn the troops were withdrawn from the fort, except for a few observation parties, and the firing totally ceased. Orders were given that in case La Mothe should approach not to alarm or fire on him without the certainty of killing or capturing the whole party. Within less than a quarter of an hour he passed within ten feet of an officer and small party of men who were lying concealed. Ladders were thrown over the walls of the fort and as they mounted them our party raised a shout. Many of them fell from the top of the wall, some inside and some outside the fort, but as we did not fire on them they all got over to the great joy of their friends. This was readily perceived by us but I had no doubt that on consideration they must be convinced that it was a stratagem of ours to let them into the fort and that we were so strong as to feel little concern for them.

While getting into the fort our men hallooed and made sport of them, at the same time withholding their fire, and our most blatant soldiers frequently told them of our stratagem and our reason for suffering them to enter the fort. This, on reflection, they must have believed;

but we knew that their knowledge of it could now do us no damage while it would serve to intimidate them. Notwithstanding, the garrison appeared much elated over the recovery of a valuable officer and party.

The firing immediately recommenced with redoubled vigor on both sides and I do not believe that more noise could possibly have been made by an equal number of men. Their shouting could not be heard amid the discharge of the muskets, and a continual line of fire around the garrison was maintained until shortly before daylight, when our troops were withdrawn to positions that had been prepared for them sixty to one hundred yards from the fort. Scarcely could a loophole be darkened by the garrison when a rifle ball would pass through it, and for them to have stood to their cannon would have entailed the useless destruction of their men. In this respect the situation of the two parties was much the same. It would have been imprudent in either to have wasted men unless some decisive stroke should require it.

Thus the attack continued until nine o'clock on the morning of the twenty-fourth. Learning that the two prisoners they had brought in the day before had a considerable number of letters with them I supposed it to be an express whose arrival we were expecting about this time and which I knew to be of the greatest importance to us as we had not received any message since our arrival in this country. Not being fully acquainted with the character of our enemy I was afraid these papers might be destroyed. To prevent this I sent a flag of truce to the garrison to demand of Governor Hamilton that he should not destroy the papers, throwing out some threats in case he should do so in the event his garrison should fall into my hands. He answered that they were not disposed to be awed into anything unbecoming British subjects. The firing was warmly renewed for a considerable space of time and we were obliged to take pains to prevent our men from exposing themselves unduly. Having refreshed themselves during the flag of truce, they were greatly animated and frequently expressed the desire to storm the fort and put an end to the post at once. This, however, would have been at this time a piece of rashness. Our troops warmed to their work and poured a heavy fire into the fort through every crack that could be discovered. Several of the garrison were wounded and it was quite impossible to stand near the embrasures.

Towards evening a flag of truce appeared with the following proposals.[45] I was greatly

[45] Hamilton's proposal, as recorded in Major Bowman's journal, was as follows: "Lt. Gov. Hamilton proposes to Col. Clark a truce for three days during which time he promises there shall be no defensive works carried on in the Garrison on condition Col. Clark shall observe on his part a like cessation of any offensive work, that he wishes to confer with Col.

at a loss to conceive what reason Governor Hamilton could have for wishing a truce of three days on such terms as he proposed. Many said it was a stratagem to obtain possession of me. I thought differently and had no idea that he entertained such a sentiment, as an act of that nature would infallibly ruin him. I was convinced he had some prospect of succor or of extricating himself from his predicament in some way. Although we had every reason to expect a reinforcement in less than three days that would at once put an end to the siege, I did not think it prudent to agree to the proposal and returned the following answer.[46]

We met at the church about eighty yards from the fort, Governor Hamilton, Major

Clark as soon as can be and further proposes that whatever may pass between them two and any other Person mutually agreed upon to be present, shall remain a secret till matters be finally concluded—as he wishes that whatever the result of their may be (it may redound) to the honor and credit of each party—If Col. Clark makes a difficulty of coming into the fort Lt. Gov. Hamilton will speak to him before the Gate."

[46] The answer is recorded in Major Bowman's journal as follows: "Col. Clark's compliments to Mr. Hamilton and begs leave to inform him that Col. Clark will not agree to any other terms than that of Mr. Hamilton's surrendering himself and Garrison Prisoners at discretion if Mr. Hamilton is desirous of a conference with Col. Clark he will meet him at the Church with Capt. Helm."

Hay[47], superintendent of Indian Affairs, Captain Helm, who was his prisoner, Major Bowman, and myself, and the conference began. Governor Hamilton produced articles of capitulation containing various provisions, one of which was that the garrison should be surrendered on being permitted to go to Pensacola on parole. After deliberating on every article I rejected the whole proposal. Hamilton then desired me to make some proposition. I told him I had no offer to make other than I had already done, that they surrender themselves as prisoners unconditionally. I observed that his troops had behaved with spirit, and without viewing us as savages they could not suppose they would be treated the worse in consequence. If he chose to comply with my demand, the sooner he should do so the better, as it was in

[47]John Hay, the detestation of whom by the Americans is well shown in the following pages, was a native of Pennsylvania who enlisted in the sixtieth American Regiment during the French and Indian War and in 1762 was sent to the Detroit frontier. He served in Pontiac's War and thereafter entered the British Indian department. In 1776, he became deputy Indian agent and major of the Detroit militia. He was Governor Hamilton's chief assistant during the latter's contest with Clark which ended with the capture of Vincennes by the Americans. Hay went with Hamilton to a Virginia dungeon and toward the close of the war he was released, and making his way to Quebec was appointed lieutenant-governor at Detroit. He had performed the duties of this office only about a year, however, when his career was cut short by death in 1785.

vain for him to make any counter proposition. He must know by this time that the fort would fall and that both of us must regard all blood that might still be spilled as murder on the part of the garrison. My troops were already impatient and begging for permission to storm the fort. If such a step were taken many of course would be cut down, and the consequences of an enraged body of woodsmen breaking into the fort must be obvious to him. It would be beyond the power of an American officer to save a single man.

Various arguments were exchanged for a considerable period of time. Captain Helm attempted to moderate my fixed determination, but I told him he was a British prisoner and it was doubtful whether he could with propriety speak on the subject. Governor Hamilton then said that Captain Helm was liberated from that moment and might act according to his pleasure. I told the Captain I would not receive him on such terms; that he must return to the fort and await his fate. I told the Governor we would not begin hostilities until a minute after the drums should give the alarm. We took leave of each other and parted, but I had gone only a few steps when the Governor stopped me and politely asked if I would be kind enough to give him my reasons for refusing any other terms than those I had offered to the garrison. I told him I had no objection to giving him my real reason, which simply was that I knew the greater part of the principal Indian partisans of Detroit were with him and I desired to be free to put them to death or treat them in any other way I might think proper. I said that the cries of the widows and the fatherless they had occasioned upon the frontiers now required their blood at my hands and I did not choose to be so timorous as to disobey the absolute command of their authority, which I regarded as next to divine. I said I would rather lose fifty men than to surrender the power properly to execute this piece of business. If he chose to risk the massacre of his garrison for their sakes it was his own affair and I might perhaps take it into my head to send for some of those widows to see it executed.

I had observed growing distrust in the countenance of Major Hay, who was paying close attention, and this in great measure influenced my conversation. Upon my concluding, "Pray, sir," said he, "who is it that you call Indian partisans?" "Sir," I replied, "I take Major Hay to be one of the principal ones." I never saw a man in the moment of execution so stricken as he appeared to be, pale and trembling, and scarcely able to stand. Governor Hamilton blushed and was, I observed, much affected at this behavior in my presence. Captain Bowman's countenance sufficiently disclosed his disdain for the one and his sorrow for the other. I viewed the whole procedure with such sentiments as I suppose are natural to some men under such circumstances. Some moments passed without a word being exchanged on either side. From that moment my resolution respecting Governor Hamilton's situation changed. I told him we would return to our respective posts when I would reconsider the matter and let him know the result. If we should decide to make any other proposal than that of surrender at discretion he should be informed of it by a flag of truce. In the contrary event, he should be on his guard at the beat of the drum. In the meantime no offensive measures should be taken. This was agreed to and we parted. On reporting to our officers what had passed at the conference it was agreed that we should modify our demands and the following articles were sent to the garrison and an answer was immediately returned. The affair being now nearly concluded troops were posted in several strong houses around the garrison and a patrol was kept up during the night to prevent any deception. The remainder of the troops not on duty lay on their arms and for the first time in many days obtained some rest.

While the conference was being held a party of about twenty warriors, who had been sent to the Falls of the Ohio for scalps and prisoners, were discovered returning. As no firing was going on at the time they entered the plain near the town, they had no suspicion of the presence of an enemy. Captain John Williams was ordered to go out to meet them. The Indians, supposing it to be a party of their friends who had come to welcome them, gave the scalp and war whoop and came on with all the parade of successful warriors. Williams' party conducted itself in like fashion. Coming closer, the Indians fired a volley in the air, to which Captain Williams replied in kind. When they were within a few steps of each other the chief stopped as if suspicious of something wrong. Captain Williams immediatley seized him, whereupon the others, perceiving their mistake, turned in flight. Fifteen of them were killed or captured, however. Two British partisans attached to their party were killed and two men who proved to be American prisoners in their hands were released. The Indians who had been taken by the soldiers were tomahawked and their bodies thrown into the river. We afterward learned that but one man of the entire party ever returned to his tribe, so that in all seventeen must have been destroyed by us. We knew that nearly all of them were badly wounded, but as we had an enemy of more importance than they were to contend with we could spare no time for pursuit, and Captain Williams allowed his men but a few minutes for executing the business before recalling them. Under these circumstances those Indians who were not killed or taken immediately got off.

One reason that I had for not wishing to receive the garrison until the following morning was that it was late in the evening before the capitulation was signed, and in view of the number of prisoners we should have in comparison with our own small force I felt the need of daylight to arrange matters to our advantage. Knowing that we could now prevent any misfortune happening, as we could now dispose our troops so as to render the fort almost useless for defense, I thought it prudent to let the British troops remain in it until morning. We should not have been so suspicious as to take so much precaution, but I must confess I could not help but doubt the honor of men who could condescend to encourage the barbarity of the Indians. Although almost every man had conceived a very favorable opinion of Governor Hamilton (and I believed that what affected myself made some impression on the whole) I was happy to find that while he stayed with us he never deviated from that conduct that became an officer in his situation.

On the morning of the twenty-fifth arrangements were made for receiving the garrison, and about ten o'clock it was surrendered with due formality and everything was immediately arranged by me to the best possible advantage. On first viewing the interior of the fort and its stores I was astonished at its being surrendered in the manner it had been. However, it was a prudent and lucky circumstance which probably saved the lives of many men on both sides since on the preceding night we had inclined to attempt to undermine it and I found it would have required great diligence on the part of the garrison to have prevented us from succeeding. I found, too, on further examination, that our information concerning the interior arrangements was so good that in all probability the first hot shot after the arrival of our artillery would have blown up the magazine. This would at once have put an end to the siege since the situation of the magazine and the quantity of powder it contained were such that its explosion must have destroyed the greater part of the garrison.

Notwithstanding our success thus far our position was still one of great difficulty. The number of prisoners we had taken, added to those of the surrendered garrison, was so considerable in comparison with our own numbers that I was at a loss so to dispose of them as not to interfere with our future operations. Detroit lay open to our attack with not more than eighty men in the fort, and a great part of these invalids. Moreover, we learned that a considerable number of the principal inhabitants were disaffected to the British cause, while the distance of the fort from any succor except at the hands of the Indians was very great. Those Indians on our route we knew would now be cooler than ever towards the

English. This matter was never rightly understood by the Government at home, or if it was, the execution of it was attempted but faintly. With Detroit in our possession and a post of communication at Cuyahoga supplies might always have been easily sent from Pittsburgh by this route and we could easily have taken possession of Lake Erie. This would have put an end to all our troubles in this quarter, and perhaps have opened the door to further advantageous operations.

Such were the ideas that influenced me at this time. We could now increase our forces in this quarter to about four hundred men since almost half of the inhabitants of Vincennes were ready to join us. Kentucky, we knew, could immediately furnish some two hundred men since it was certain that section would receive a large number of settlers in the spring. Our own stores, which we had learned were being forwarded in safety, taken in conjunction with those of the British, would leave not a single article wanting for such an attempt and supplies of provisions might be had for some time at Detroit. I privately resolved to embrace without delay the object that seemed to court my acceptance, giving the enemy no time to recover from the blows he had already received. But before saying anything about this I wished it to become an object of desire to the soldiers and townsmen. It became at once the common topic of conversation among them, and within a few days matters were so arranged that in imagination they were almost ready to march. The employment of such conversation was discountenanced by me and steps were taken to make it appear that such an attempt was foreign to my plans, while at the same time every step was taken to bring about the result I desired. The quantity of public goods brought from Detroit by Governor Hamilton, added to what had belonged to the traders of Vincennes whom we had captured, was very great. The entire amount was immediately divided among the soldiers with the exception of some Indian medals, which were retained to be of some public use.. The officers received nothing except a few articles of clothing of which they stood in need. The soldiers were laden with wealth and the townsmen envied their good fortune and wished some enterprise might be undertaken which would enable them to do something.

Detroit was their goal and the clamor now rose to a great height. To silence it, and at the same time to answer other purposes, I told them that an army was to march the coming summer from Pittsburgh against Detroit, although from last autumn's proceedings I knew nothing of the sort was to be apprehended. An entire company of Captain La Mothe's volunteers from Detroit, mostly composed of young men, was drawn up. While they were anticipating being sent into a strange country with the probability of never returning to their homes, I told them we were happy to learn that many of them had been torn from their fathers and mothers and forced to go on this expedition; while others, ignorant of the true issue at stake, had engaged in the conflict in obedience to a principle which actuates many men, that of being fond of adventure. They had now enjoyed a good opportunity, however, of acquainting themselves fully with the character of the war, which they were now in a position to explain to their friends. Since we knew that to send them to the States, where they would be confined in jail, probably for the duration of the war, would make a large number of our friends at Detroit unhappy we had thought proper for their sakes to permit them to return home.

Much was said to them along this line; after which they were discharged in a body upon taking an oath not to bear arms against America until exchanged, and I issued an order for their arms and boats to be returned to them, together with provisions for the return journey. Upon their arrival at home the boats were to be sold and the proceeds divided among them. Within a few days they set out and from our spies who went among them as traders we learned that they played havoc with the British interests on their return, stating publicly that while they had taken an oath not to fight against America they had taken none to refrain from fighting for us. Things were carried with such a high hand by them that the commanding officer thought it prudent to take no notice of anything that was said or done. Mrs. McComb, who kept a noted boarding house, had the assurance, I was told, to show the commander the stores she had provided for the Americans. Thus was realized the design I had had in view in permitting this company to return. Many others whom we could trust were permitted to enlist in the corps, so that our burden of prisoners was much reduced.

Learning that ten boat loads of goods and provisions were daily expected to descend the Wabash and fearing they would gain intelligence of the situation at Vincennes and turn back, on the twenty-sixth of the month I sent Captain Helm, Major Bosseron[48] and Major Le Gras[49] with fifty volunteers in three armed

[48] François Bosseron was one of the most prominent citizens of Vincennes. He was enrolled in the British militia forces, but on the advent of the Americans gave them his hearty support. He served with Captain Helms in the Wabash expedition of 1779, and furnished ammunition for the invading army. He was later district commandant and territorial judge, dying at Vincennes in 1791. A street in Vincennes still bears his name.

[49] J. M. P. Le Gras was a prominent merchant of Vincennes who had served as captain of militia under the British regime. He sided with the Americans upon the advent of Clark in Illinois and by Clark was made major and later colonel of militia. In June, 1779, he was appointed president of the local court at Vincennes.

boats in pursuit of them. On the twenty-seventh our galley arrived safely with the crew much mortified over their failure to be in time, although they were deserving of great credit for their diligence. On their passage they had overtaken William Myers with an express from the Government at home. The dispatches he brought gave us great encouragement, representing that our own battalion was to be completed and an additional one was to come out in the spring. On first reading this gave us both pleasure and pain but in the end resulted to our disadvantage. I had but a day or two in which to consider the situation and fix on a plan of operations. Should we make the attempt on Detroit without delay we were almost certain of success, since we knew our own strength and supplies and lacked no information concerning that post. On the other hand, we were now flattered with the prospect of an immediate reinforcement.

A council was convened on the subject. I laid before the officers my plans for the immediate reduction of Detroit and explained the practical certainty of success and the probability of our retaining possession of the place until they could secure succor from the States. This we might reasonably expect they would bend every effort to send us on receiving the news of the capture, which we could easily convey to them in a few weeks. On the other hand, if we awaited the arrival of the troops mentioned in the dispatch the enemy might meanwhile be reinforced, and we might not be as well prepared to carry the place with the addition of the expected reinforcement as we should be with our present force in case we were to make the attempt now; while in the event of being disappointed in receiving the promised reinforcements we might not be able to effect it at all.

Various arguments were employed over this delicate question. Every one appeared anxious to embrace the present opportunity while prudence seemed to forbid our proceeding without awaiting the reinforcement. The argument which appeared to have the greatest weight was that with such a force we might march boldly through the Indian country, and that this would produce a greater effect on the natives as well as on the inhabitants of Detroit than if we should slip off with our present small force and take the place which was certainly in our power. It was urged that the British would not care to weaken Niagara by sending any considerable reinforcement to Detroit; that it was more difficult for them to receive aid from Canada than it was for us to obtain it from the States; and that they would be unable to obtain reinforcements in time to prevent the execution of our design, since we might reasonably expect our help to arrive within a few weeks. In short, the enterprise was postponed until the   of June when we were to rendezvous at this post. In the meantime provisions were to be procured and all possible preparations made for the enterprise; while to conceal our design our whole force at Vincennes, with the exception of a small garrison, should immediately return to the Illinois while orders were sent to the Kentuckians to hold themselves in readiness to meet with us at the appointed time. This was now our plan, in accordance with which our operations the ensuing spring should be conducted.

On the fifth of March Captain Helm and Majors Bosseron and Le Gras returned from their tour up river, having met with great success. They had come upon the enemy in the night and, observing their fires at a distance, had waited until all was quiet, when the camp was surrounded and the entire force captured without firing a gun. These men had felt so secure and entertained so little apprehension of an enemy being in that part of the world they could hardly persuade themselves that what they heard and saw was real. It proved a valuable capture, comprising seven boats loaded with a considerable quantity of provisions and goods. The provisions were taken for public use, while the goods were divided among our men, with the exception of about eight hundred pounds worth which I reserved to clothe the troops we expected shortly to receive. This was quite agreeable to the soldiers since I told them the state would pay them their share in money and they had an ample supply of goods. The reservation I made proved useful, for the few troops that came to us were on their arrival almost naked.

On March 7 Captains Williams and Rogers with a party of twenty-five men set out by water to conduct the British officers to Kentucky; while eighteen privates were sent along to reduce further the number of prisoners in our hands. Captain Rogers was instructed upon their arrival at the Falls to superintend their journey to Williamsburg, take care that ample supplies should be furnished them enroute, and on arrival to await the orders of the Governor. Poor Myers was killed on the return journey and his dispatches fell into the hands of the enemy; but I had been so much on my guard that there was no sentence in them which could harm us for the enemy to know, while the private letters from the soldiers to their friends at home were designed rather with a view to deception in the event of such an accident. This was customary with us as our expresses were frequently surprised. I sent a second dispatch to the Governor, giving him a short but full account of what had transpired and my views concerning the situation. My copy of this message has long been lost, along with many other papers, but I suppose the original can be found among the public papers of this period. I sent letters, also, to the commandant of Kentucky, directing him to give me a correct but secret account of the number of men he could furnish in June.

The weather being now very disagreeable, and having some leisure, our time was spent in consultation and in arranging matters to the best advantage. A number of our men now became sick. Their intrepidity and our success had kept up their spirits hitherto; but our activities now falling off to little more than garrison duty, they became more sensible of the pains and other complaints which had been contracted during the severity of our uncommon march. To these many of those valuable men succumbed while but few of the remainder ever entirely recovered.

As yet I had sent no message to the Indian tribes, preferring to wait to see what effect all that had happened would have on them. The Piankashaw, being of the tribe of the Tobacco's son, had all along been friendly with us. Some of the behavior of this grandee, as he regarded himself, was diverting enough. He had conceived such a violent attachment to Colonel Helm that on finding the latter a prisoner and we not being able as yet to release him, he declared himself a prisoner also and joined his brother as he called him, remaining continually with him and condoling over their condition as prisoners in great distress, although at the same time nothing was wanting to them which it was within the power of the garrison to supply. Governor Hamilton, knowing his influence, was extremely jealous of his behavior and employed every pains, by the giving of presents, etc., to win him over. When anything was presented him, however, he would reply that it would serve him and his brother to live on and would refuse to enter into council, saying that he was a prisoner and had nothing to say, but that he was in hopes that when the grass grew again his brothers, the Big Knives, would release him and then he would be free to talk. Being presented with an elegant sword, he drew it, and bending the point on the floor, said very seriously that it would serve himself and his brother to amuse themselves sticking frogs while they were in captivity. In short, they could do nothing with him and the moment he heard of our arrival he paraded all the warriors he had in his village (which adjoined Vincennes) and was eager to join us in the attack on the fort, but for the reasons already noted I desired him to refrain.

On the fifteenth a party of Chippewa, of upper Piankashaw, Potawatomi, and Miami, made their appearance, making great protestations of their attachment to the Americans. They begged to be taken under the cover of our wings, and that the roads through their land might be made straight and all the stumbling blocks removed; and they asked that their friends, the neighboring nations, might also be regarded in the same light. I well knew from what principle all this sprang, and as my eye was now fixed on Detroit it was my concern to make a clear road for myself to walk in without giving much thought to their interest or anything else but the opening of this road, whether by flattery, deception, or any other means. I told them I was glad to see them and was happy to learn that most of the tribes on the Wabash and Miami Rivers had proved themselves to be men last fall by adhering strictly to the treaties they had with the Big Knives, with the exception of a few weak minds who had been deluded by the English into waging war against us. I said I did not know exactly who they were nor did I much care, but that I understood they were a band composed of the off-scouring of almost all the tribes; that such people, mean enough to sell their country for a shirt, were to be found among all nations but since they were not worthy the attention of warriors we would say no more about them, but turn to subjects more becoming to us. I told them I would let the great Council of the Americans know of their behavior and that I knew they would be counted as friends of the Big Knives, who would always keep them under their protection and safeguard their country for them since the Big Knives had land enough and did not want any more; but if they should ever break their faith the Big Knives would never trust them again since they never retain friendship with a people whom they find to have two hearts. I said they were witnesses to the calamities the British had brought upon them by their false assertions and their presents, which were a sufficient proof of their weakness. They had seen all the boasted valor of the British fall to the ground and that they did not come out of their fort the other day to save the Indians they had flattered to war and now suffered to be killed in their sight. As the nature of the war had been fully explained to them last fall they might clearly see that the Great Spirit did not suffer it otherwise. Not only was this the case on the Wabash but everywhere else as well. They might rest assured that the tribes which continued obstinately to listen to the English would be driven out of the country and their land given to those who where steadfast friends of the Americans. I said I expected for the future that if any of my people should be going to war through their country they would be protected, which would always be the case with their people when among us, and that mutual confidence should continue to exist between us.

They replied that they were convinced from what they had seen and heard that the Master of Life had a hand in all things. They said their people would rejoice on their return, and that they would take pains to diffuse what they had heard throughout all the tribes and they had no doubt of the good it would produce. After a long speech in the Indian fashion, calling all the spirits as witnesses, they concluded by renewing the chain of friendship, smoking the sacred pipe, and exchanging belts with us; and I believe they went off really well pleased, although unable to fathom all they had heard, the greater part of which was merely political lies. During the ensuing summer Captain J. Shelby with his single company lay for a considerable time in the Wea town in the heart of their country. He was treated in the most friendly manner by all the natives he saw, being frequently invited by them to join them in plundering what they called the King's pasture at Detroit. By this they meant to go and steal horses from that settlement. About this time an express arrived from the Illinois with letters from Captain Robert George.[50]

Matters being now pretty well arranged, I

[50] At this point in the original manuscript a blank half page occurs, together with the marginal note, "Inquire of Captain George, J. R. C."

Robert George is believed to have been a cousin of Clark. He was in the West as a trader as early as 1777, and in 1778 accompanied Captain James Willings' expedition to the lower Mississippi. Early in 1779 Willing sent him up the Mississippi with forty men to join Clark, and the party arrived at Kaskaskia while Clark was still at Vincennes. George remained in the West until the close of the Revolution. He later settled on Clark's grant in Indiana, and died there some time prior to 1800.

[51] Richard Brashers was originally one of Captain William Howard's company, who probably came from Pennsylvania.

appointed Lieutenant Richard Brashers[51] to the command of the garrison, consisting of Lieutenants Bailey[52] and Chapline[53] and forty picked

[52] John Bailey came to Kentucky from Virginia in 1776, and in 1778 joined Clark's expedition against the Illinois towns. In August Clark sent him to the aid of Captain Helm at Vincennes. Returning to Kaskaskia, Bailey accompanied Clark on his winter march against Vincennes, and was sent in advance with a detachment of fourteen men to begin the attack on the British post. Upon Clark's leaving Vincennes Bailey was left behind as here noted in command of a post of the garrison. In 1780 he served in Montgomery's Rock River expedition, and during most of 1781 he was serving as commandant, under great difficulties, at Vincennes. At the close of the Revolution he became a Baptist preacher, and helped lay the foundations of that church in Kentucky. In 1792 and again in 1799 he served in Kentucky constitutional conventions, and voted in favor of an emancipation clause. He died in Lincoln country in 1816.

[53] Abraham Chapline was a native of Virginia, who in 1774 at an early age came to Kentucky in Captain James Harrod's party. In the autumn of this year he took part in the battle of Point Pleasant, and the next year returned to Kentucky. He joined Clark's Illinois expedition and by the leader was made an ensign and later a lieutenant. Detailed to escort Colonel Rogers' party to Fort Pitt, Chapline was captured at its defeat and taken by the Indians to the head waters of the Big Miami River. Here he was forced to run the gauntlet and then adopted into an Indian family. He later escaped, served until the end of the war, and then settled in Mercer Country, Kentucky. He practiced medicine and served in the Kentucky legislature. He died on his farm near Harrodsburg in January, 1824.

men. I made Captain Helm commandant of the town and Superintendent of Indian Affairs and having given the necessary instructions to all those whom I left in office, on the 20th of March, with seventy men, I set sail on board our galley, which had now been made perfectly complete, attended by five armed boats. The water being very high, we soon reached the Missouri, and with favoring winds we arrived in a few days at Kaskaskia to the great joy of our new friends, Captain George and company, who were waiting to receive us.

On our passage up the Mississippi we observed several Indian camps which appeared to us to be recent and to have been abandoned in great confusion. We had been unable to account for this but we were now informed that a few days since a party of Delaware warriors had gone to town and acted very impudently. In the evening, having indulged in drink, they swore they had come for scalps and meant to have them, and flashed a gun at the breast of an American woman who was present. A sergeant and party passing the house at the moment saw the confusion and entered. The Indians immediately fled. The sergeant pursued and killed   of them. A party was instantly sent to rout them from their camps on the river. This had been done the day before we came up, which was the occasion of the sign we had seen. A portion of the Delaware nation had settled a town at the forks of White River and they hunted over the region adjacent to the Ohio and the Mississippi rivers. On our first arrival in the country they had hatched up a sort of peace with us. I knew all along, however, that they desired open war, but never before this could I gain a proper excuse for exterminating them from the country. This I knew they would be loath to leave, and also that the other Indians wished them driven off as they were great hunters and killed off their game.

A few days after this Captain Helm informed me by express that a party of traders going by land to the Falls of the Ohio had been plundered and killed by the Delawares of White River; and that their designs appeared altogether hostile as they had received a belt from the great council of their tribe. I was sorry for the loss of our men but for the rest pleased over what had happened, since it would afford me an opportunity of showing the other Indians the horrible fate of those who dared to make war on the Big Knives; and I knew that to excel them in barbarity was and is the only way to make war upon Indians and gain a name among them. I immediately sent orders to Vincennes to make war on the Delawares and to use every means in our power to destroy them, showing no mercy to the men, but sparing the women and children. This order was executed without delay. Their camps were attacked wherever they could be found, Many were slain, while others were brought to Vincennes and there put to death and the women and children taken captive. They immediately begged for peace but were told that I had ordered the war for reasons which were explained to them and that our men dare not lay down the tomahawk without my permission; but if the Indians should agree upon it, no more blood would be spilled until an express could be sent to me at Kaskaskia. I refused to make peace with the Delawares, telling them that we never trusted those who had once violated their faith; but if they were disposed to be quiet and if they could induce any of the neighboring Indians to be responsible for their good behavior I would let them alone, although I cared little what they might do.

A council was called by Captain Helm (whom I had privately instructed how to manage the matter) of all the Indians in the neighborhood, at which my answer was made public. The Piankashaw undertook to answer for the future good conduct of the Delawares, and the son of Tobacco in a long speech told them how base their conduct had been, and how richly they had deserved the severe blow which had fallen upon them. He reminded them that he had given them permission to settle in this country but not to kill his friends. They now saw that the Big Knives had refused to make peace with them and that he had become surety for their good conduct. They might go now and attend to their hunting but if they should ever do any more mischief—he concluded with a significant gesture to the sacred bow[54] he held in his left hand; this was as much as to say that for the future he himself would chastise them. Thus the war with the Delawares in this country ended greatly to our advantage, with the neighboring tribes saying we were as brave as Indians and not afraid to put our enemy to death.

A rendezvous at this post having been set for the month of June, we exerted ourselves diligently procuring provisions of all kinds and making other preparations. Meanwhile I received an express from Colonel Bowman in Kentucky, informing me that he could furnish three hundred good men. We were now going on in high spirits and daily expecting the troops down the Ohio when on the we were surprised at the arrival of Colonel Montgomery with only one hundred and fifty men. He brought the information that we could expect no men from that quarter in the near future, if indeed at all, as the recruiting business proceeded but slowly, and I now learned for the

[54] In the original manuscript Clark has placed this marginal note; "This bow is decorated with beautiful feathers (from) an Eagle's tail and all the gaudy trinkets that can be put about it and at one end is a spear about six inches dipt in blood which he touched when he shewed (it) to the Delawares except the Pipe of Peace this is the most sacred Instrument known to the Inds. and only handled by those of the greatest dignity."—G. R. C.

first time of the depreciation of our paper money. Our affairs at once assumed a different aspect. We now regretted that we had not marched from Vincennes upon Detroit at once, but as we still had the prospect of receiving considerable reinforcements from Kentucky we flattered ourselves that something might yet be accomplished; that at the least we might maneuver in such fashion as to keep the enemy in hot water and to prevent his doing our frontier much damage.

We continued the work of procuring supplies and did not as yet lose sight of our object. To feel the pulse of the enemy I sent a company of volunteers under Linctot,[55] who had recently joined us, up the Illinois River under the pretense of visiting our friends, to cross the country and fall upon the Wea towns, returning thence

[55] Major Godefroy de Linctot was one of two French officers of the same name who at the close of the French and Indian War established themselves as traders in the Northwest with headquarters at Cahokia. Whether they were brothers or father and son is not entirely clear. One of them died during the winter of 1778. The other, here mentioned, attached himself to the American cause when Clark came into Illinois, and as Clark's agent had much success in winning the various Indian tribes away from their British alliance. The appointment to the Illinois River expedition, here described, followed. That Detroit was not taken was no fault of Linctot, who had performed successfully the preliminary movement assigned him. He continued in the American interest until after his death, which seems to have occured in 1781.

to Vincennes to report upon the observations he had made. This maneuver, I anticipated, would suffice to cover our own designs and if we should think it prudent upon his return, we might proceed against Detroit early in June.

Colonel Montgomery was sent on by water with the whole of our stores. Major Bowman marched the remainder of our troops by land, while I, with a party of horsemen, reached Vincennes in four days' time, and the whole force arrived safely a short time afterwards. But instead of three hundred men from Kentucky there now appeared about thirty volunteers commanded by Captain McGary.[56] The loss of the expedition was too obvious to hesitate over. Colonel Bowman[57] had turned his attention against the Shawnee town and had

[56] Hugh McGary was one of the first settlers of Harrodsburg. Aside from the service here noted he served in Clark's expedition into Ohio in the summer of 1780, when Old Chillicothe and Piqua were destroyed.

[57] Colonel John Bowman, whose career has been previously noted, in the spring of 1779, led 296 men in an attack upon the Shawnee town of Chillicothe. The Indians fortified themselves in some log cabins and fought so vigorously that Bowman's force was repulsed. They burned most of the town and retired with much plunder, but for want of their cooperation Clark was forced to forego attacking Detroit, according to Captain Patten, who was with Bowman. The Americans captured a negro woman who informed them that the Indians had sent a runner to Simon Girty, the notorious Tory, who was at the Pickaway

been repulsed and his men had become discouraged.

From the first the affair I had in hand had been so conducted as to produce no disadvantageous impression upon the enemy in case of a disappointment, since they could never know whether we ever really entertained a design upon Detroit or were only making a feint to amuse them. To arrange matters to the best possible advantage was now my principal study. Part of the troops were sent to the Falls of the Ohio and the remainder divided among the posts of Vincennes, Cahokia, and Kaskaskia. I appointed Colonel Montgomery to the command of the Illinois. I authorized Major Bowman to superintend the recruiting business and appointed a number of officers to this service. Major Linctot and Captain Helm were given the superintendence of Indian Affairs, while I myself took station at the Falls as the most convenient spot from which to supervise the whole field. Having departed for their several posts in August I set off by land, proceeding in a few days as far as White River.[58]

town with one hundred Mingos. On hearing this Colonel Bowman ordered his force to begin the retreat. Captain Patten records that he was "a good citizen but not aquainted with Indian warfare." The summer following Bowman's repulse Clark burned both Chillicothe and Piqua.

[58]The manuscript is imperfect at this point. In Clark's letter to George Mason, November 19, 1779,

Our movement during the summer had confused the enemy. The officer in command at Michilimackinac had therefore sent an expedition into the Illinois country by way of St. Joseph to drive out the American traders. Arriving at St. Joseph while Major Linctot was on his way up the Illinois River, it was reported that an American army was approaching and the Indians immediately deserted the English. On being asked the reason for this action they replied that they had been invited to see the English and the Big Knives fight and since the fight was now in prospect they had withdrawn to a height in order to enjoy a full view of it. The English, realizing that no dependence could be placed on the Indians, withdrew to the mouth of the St. Joseph River and there established a strong camp. On first receiving the intelligence of Linctot's advance they had sent off an express to Mackinac. A sloop dispatched from that place with provisions for the troops came within full view of their camp at the mouth of the river; but supposing it to be the Americans who had captured their friends at St. Joseph and taken post there, the vessel ignored all the signs they made and returned to Mackinac with the disagreeable news, leaving the poor fellows to starve until they could get an answer to a second express. In the

he states, concerning this period: "After giving proper Instructions for the discretion of the Conds. of the different posts I set out for the falls where I arrived safe on the 20 day of August."

meantime Mr. Linctot, knowing nothing of all this, had changed his route to the Wea town, which caused the English to conjecture that our whole force was being directed against Detroit, producing great confusion among them.

The summer was spent profitably, as we were careful to spread abroad such reports as suited our interests. I remained at Louisville until the following spring, discharging the multiplicity of business that was continually brought to me from every quarter. I represented to the Governor of Virginia that as the new settlers now peopling Kentucky were quite numerous, I hoped they were fully able to withstand any force the enemy could send against her and perhaps to act on the offensive. We now began to feel the effects of the depreciated state of the paper currency. Everything was two or three times the normal price, and scarcely to be had upon any terms. We engaged this fall upon the plan of laying up great quantities of jerked meat for the following season; but as the English at Detroit had pretty well recovered themselves the Shawnee, Delaware, and other Indian tribes were so troublesome that our hunters met with no success. Many of them were cut off and small skirmishes became so common throughout the region as to excite but slight attention. Captain Rogers, who had been sent to the Mississippi for a considerable quantity of goods and had obtained a reinforcement at the Falls, was totally defeated a little above Licking Creek on his return to Pittsburgh, and almost all of his party of seventy men were killed or made prisoners. Among the latter the more important were Colonel John Campbell and Captain Abraham Chapline. Of all the expedition, but one small boat made its escape.

Index

Index

Index

Index

Index

Index

Index

Index

Index

Index

Index

Index